nomenclature & hierarchy

basic latin american legal sources

by
Rubens Medina
and
Cecilia Medina-Quiroga

With the editorial assistance
of Sandra A. Sawicki

Library of Congress Washington 1979

Library of Congress Cataloging in Publication Data

Medina, Rubens.
Nomenclature and hierarchy–basic Latin American legal sources, Library of Congress.

1. Law–Latin America–Sources–Bibliography.
2. Legal research–Latin America. 3. Law–Latin America–Terms and phrases. I. Medina Quiroga, Cecilia, joint author. II. Title.
Law 016.34'0098 79-14005
ISBN 0-8444-0311-3

For sale by the Superintendent of Documents, U.S. Government Printing Office
Washington, D.C. 20402

Stock Number 030-013-00008-5

Foreword

The Library of Congress Law Library is the largest and most comprehensive repository of legal materials in the world, containing over 1.6 million volumes which cover the full panoply of national legal systems and, in addition, Roman law, canon law, and ancient and medieval law. The resources and information in its possession are made accessible to a divergent clientele–Congress, the executive and judicial branches of government, research organizations, the bench and bar, and other sectors of the scholarly, law, and library communities –through various mediums which include written reports, telephone responses, bibliographies, translations, guides, indexes, digests, and publications.

As part of its publishing program, the Law Library has prepared this guide in response to a need frequently voiced by researchers studying the legal processes in the nations of Latin America. Their repeated tendency to link similarly titled legal instruments, such as decree law and executive decree, from such different jurisdictions as Mexico, Argentina, or Colombia is misdirected and hinders them from making proper judgments about the legal mechanisms in these countries. In recent years the specialists of the Hispanic Law Division conceived the idea of a reference manual identifying and explaining the nomenclature and hierarchy of twenty Latin jurisdictions. Serious work on the project began in 1977. As far as can be ascertained, no other guide of this type dealing with basic Hispanic legal sources has ever been published. The authors, therefore, are deserving of exceptional praise in applying themselves to this problem and filling a very evident gap in foreign legal research aides.

Rubens Medina, Chief of the Hispanic Law Division, received his legal education and training in his native Paraguay. In 1964 he came to the United States to pursue advanced legal research and study under fellowships from the University of Wisconsin's Land Tenure Center, Law School, and International Studies Program, and from the Organization of American States. He received an M.S. in legal institutions and a Ph.D. in law and sociology from Wisconsin. His teaching credentials include professorships at the School of Law of the Catholic University of Valparaiso, Chile, the University of Wisconsin Law School, and the Chile Law Program at New York University Law School. He has held his current position since 1971.

His coauthor, Cecilia Medina-Quiroga is a lawyer and legal scholar from Chile. She graduated from the School of Law of the University of Chile in Santiago and then later became a full professor of constitutional law at the same university. Ms. Medina-Quiroga practiced law privately in Chile and held official positions in the government. As a legal research assistant with a temporary appointment to the Hispanic Law Division, she conducted research and collaborated on this project. Both Dr. Medina and Ms. Medina-Quiroga have previously published several legal papers and studies.

Carleton W. Kenyon
Law Librarian of Congress

preface

Researchers in the fields of foreign, comparative, and international law frequently confront the problems of nomenclature and hierarchy of basic statutory sources. Difficulty in nomenclature arises when designations which are very similar or identical to those with which the researcher is familiar are used for statutory or regulatory instruments in one or more foreign jurisdictions. This difficulty is heightened when foreign jurisdictions whose language is the same, for instance the eighteen nations of Latin America where Spanish is spoken, place seemingly similar or identical designations on their legal instruments. Generally this similarity or identicalness of designation or name is only verbal. Unfortunately the researcher may be misled to assume that the word or phrase in question matches the nomenclature of his or her own country. In all likelihood, the researcher will mistakenly impose the hierarchical scheme with which he or she is more familiar upon the foreign legal system being examined.

The other prevalent problem of the foreign law researcher is that statutory and regulatory texts often amend or contradict previous instruments, but these statutory texts do not always make reference to the instruments being amended or repealed. With instruments of the same designation chronology will determine which is the prevailing text. But when amendatory or derogatory texts are found in instruments of different designations the correct judgment can only be made in accordance with the scheme of hierarchy governing each legal system. An awareness of these characteristics of foreign legal sources is critical for a true assessment of the status of the law in any given jurisdiction, especially with regard to the accuracy and currency of the texts concerned.

This work is intended to be an instrument for researchers exposed to such problems since dictionaries and other general reference sources have proved inadequate, according to the experience of many scholars with whom the authors have had the opportunity to work or exchange ideas. This project was limited to the basic instruments of legislative and high executive issuance in the eighteen Hispanic nations of Latin America, Brazil, and Haiti.

This guide does not cover instruments issued by medium- and low-level executive agencies, the courts, commissions, boards, and such autonomous and semiautonomous official entities as the central banks, customs houses, and police departments, on which special regulatory powers are vested. Although the authors are aware of the critical importance of these lower ranking instruments, especially when preparing material for the adjudication of the courts, they excluded them simply because of limitations imposed by the time and resources assigned to the project and because this reference text was intended to be made available to users without delay.

The jurisdictions covered here were not selected in accordance with any rigorous theoretical criteria but as a simple response to the daily work demands and jurisdictional assignments of the Hispanic Law Division of the Law Library, Library of Congress. The jurisdictions are presented in alphabetical order.

The hierarchical scheme of each legal system is indicated by the sequential order observed, beginning with the highest ranking instrument, which in Latin America is invariably the constitution. In those instances where there is more than one instrument within a given rank this is indicated.

At an early stage of the study, the authors encountered the "black letter law," or law in the book, versus law in action, or de facto law, dichotomy. This situation required consulting thousands of issues of the countries' official gazettes in which all instruments, prescribed or de facto, were almost invariably printed. The authors decided to present the information concerning the de facto instruments immediately following the description of the equivalent "officially" designated statute or regulation under the subtitle, "Current Status."

To aid the researcher further, the authors have devised a chart for each jurisdiction which appears before each country's chapter and which shows clearly and at a glance the ranking of legislative and high executive issuances. Instruments are numbered in descending order from one to five, the highest ranking instrument being number one. Instruments with different designations but equal rank are listed laterally after the same number. For those countries where de facto law has replaced the system prescribed by the constitution, two charts are given, the first entitled, "Under the Constitution," and the second, "Current Status."

The most common source of relevant information is the national charter of each jurisdiction. In most cases the constitution includes a special chapter or section on the legislative process and names the basic instruments to be issued by the branches of the state in the exercise of their assigned lawmaking powers. Nevertheless, the general nature of these fundamental texts required expansion and interpretation by the authors, for which they consulted related statutes, court decisions, legal monographs, law journals, and scholarly reports.

The methodology for analysis was frequently frustrated by the dearth of written matter on legal processes in some countries and by the sheer lack of any information in others. In these cases the authors have provided the reader not only a conceptual definition of each designation but a formal description and functional analysis as well. The task was not easy.

The authors express their gratitude to Sandra A. Sawicki, legal research assistant of the Hispanic Law Division, for the efficient and painstaking support she provided during the project to bring the manuscript to publishable form.

The authors hope that the results of their work, consigned in the following pages, will benefit and instruct researchers interested in foreign legal materials.

contents

ARGENTINA

Under the Constitution

1. Constitution
2. Law   Treaties
3. Regulatory Decree
4. Decree

Current Status

1. Constitution   Acts   Statutes
2. Law   Treaties   Decree (*Junta de Gobierno*)
3. Regulatory Decree
4. Decree

ARGENTINA

CONSTITUCIÓN (Constitution). This nation is politically organized as a federation of provinces. The national charter provides that the constitution, laws of the nation enacted by congress in pursuance thereof, and treaties with foreign powers are the supreme laws of the nation.[1] The national constitution has hierarchical priority over all other legislative instruments.

Consonant with the above principle, the charter further provides that it may be amended only by strictly observing the specific procedural norms set forth in the constitution itself. According to such norms, amendments to the charter may be either total or partial. The first procedural step to be taken is the issuance of a congressional declaration that an amendment is required. This declaration must contain concrete and direct references to the passage or passages to be amended or a statement concerning the need for total reform. This issuance is made as an ordinary congressional enactment but requires the support of at least two-thirds of the membership's favorable votes.[2]

When bills concerning constitutional amendments are submitted, congressional action, consisting of debating and approving, is not by itself sufficient to enact the amendment. It is further required that a constituent convention be convened. No references were found concerning the organizational and functional aspects of the convention in the constitution or in the related statutes available. Commentaries by a well-known national scholar, however, indicate that congress ordinarily passes a law to cover these aspects of the convention. He suggests that the convention itself is thereafter empowered to issue whatever regulation is necessary for the fulfillment of its specific objectives.[3]

The current constitutional text of Argentina was orginally enacted on May 1, 1853. The original version was subject to a number of amendments, the last ones being the result of the *Estatuto para el proceso de reorganización nacional* (Statute for the Process of National Reorganization) enacted by the military junta in power.[4] This statute is in fact currently predominant over the charter itself.

Current Status. The commanders general of the army, navy, and air force seized control of the Argentine government on March 24, 1976, and established themselves as a military junta. The national congress was dissolved, the president of the republic was ousted as well as the justices of the supreme court and a number of high provincial government officials. Immediately thereafter the military junta issued an instrument which set forth the basic objectives of an alleged national process of reorganization.[5] Another instrument containing the basic norms to rule the country was enacted on March 31, 1976, by the military junta in exercise of the constituent powers assumed thereby.[6]

Despite the severe impact of the above instrument on the more relevant provisions of the national charter the new enactment stated that the national constitution of 1853 was thereby declared to continue in force "to the extent that it did not oppose the main objectives set forth by the military junta or the provisions of the statute itself."[7] The junta proclaimed itself the "supreme organ of the nation," an investiture that was later reaffirmed by an instrument issued to govern the performance of the military junta, the national executive power, and the Legislative Advisory Committee.[8]

Under the current circumstances, the constituent power is held by the military junta. Neither general nor specific provisions have been located containing references to the manner in which this power is to be exercised by the junta. A review of the 1976 issues of the official gazette suggested that in practice this exercise most probably was effected by means of certain instruments designated *actas* (acts) and *estatutos* (statutes). They are published in the official gazette under the signatures of the commander generals of the military junta and directly under the headings of Acts and Statutes.

The military junta also issues a third category of instrument designated as decrees. These instruments usually contain provisions controlling matters of lesser relevance and are, therefore, subordinate to the acts and the statutes. However, some decrees bear provisions on civil rights and a number of other subjects related to basic constitutional guarantees.

LEY (Law). This instrument results directly from exercising the legislative power entrusted by the charter to the Argentine Congress, an elected body composed of two chambers, the Senate and the Chamber of Deputies or Representatives. Despite this apparent specific and exclusive assignment, the chief executive has also been assigned a relevant participatory role in the lawmaking process by the charter.[10]

Ordinarily bills are submitted to either of the congressional chambers by their corresponding members or by initiative of the executive branch, that is, the president and his cabinet ministers,[11] but such specific bills as those concerning taxation and military draft require submission before the Chamber of Deputies exclusively.[12]

Bills are debated and voted upon in both chambers. If approved, they are forwarded to the executive branch for promulgation or veto by the president of the nation within ten days.[13] If vetoed, bills are returned to the Congress for further debating and voting by both chambers, at which time the favorable vote of a special majority of two-thirds of the respective memberships is required for congressional approval. In this regard, the wording of the corresponding constitutional passage does not clearly state whether this special majority is required to override the presidential veto, to go along with it, or both. Works by national authors failed to shed light on the question. After the vetoed bill is approved, it is again forwarded to the president for promulgation. A national author observed from the contents of the official gazette that this formality is performed by a decree signed by the president and the corresponding minister of the cabinet.[14] Commentaries on the topic by this national author state that should the president fail to act within the prescribed term the bill is, in practice, automatically considered tacitly promulgated.[15]

According to a specific provision of the constitution, all laws enacted must be headed by the statement, "The Senate and the Chamber of Deputies of the Argentine nation, assembled in Congress, sanction with the force of law . . . ."[16] Enforceability is dependent upon publication of the instrument. Laws take effect eight days after their publication in the *Boletín Oficial,* the Argentine official gazette, unless otherwise stated in the law itself.[17]

Concerning the hierarchical rank of the laws, they are directly subordinate to the national charter.[18]

Examination of official legislative sources reveals that there have been times during which the Argentine Congress delegated its legislative prerogatives to the president of the republic, a rather curious situation since no references to this effect were found either in the charter itself or in any of the related statutes. Notwithstanding, when this delegation takes place the president issues decrees which, consonant with the original congressional enactment, carry the force of law. These instruments may occasionally be found in the official gazette under the decree heading.

Current Status. Under the terms of the Statute for the Process of National Reorganization, most legislative functions are currently vested in the president of the republic, the remaining ones are entrusted to the military junta.[19] The Legislative Advisory Committee participates in the law making process in a consulting capacity. Its membership is composed of high ranking officers from the armed forces.[20] Regulation on the procedures to be observed for the enactment of laws were promulgated in 1976. In this regard, bills are submitted to the Legislative Advisory Committee either by the president of the nation or by the commander generals of the armed forces. When the committee decides to assign one of the bills submitted to the category of "significantly important," it retains the bill for further studies. Once these are completed, they are attached to the bill concerned and returned to the executive branch with the committee's opinion. If the executive disagrees, the bill is forwarded to the military junta for a final decision on whether or not to promulgate.[21]

Ordinary bills are simply put through routine channels by the committee. They are sanctioned and promulgated by the executive without delay. Examination of the content of official gazettes indicates that laws are sanctioned and promulgated in one document which also contained the text of the statute concerned.

Laws are published in the official gazette preceded by a message. According to observations this message is used to introduce the bill before the executive. Sources consulted and several issues of the official gazette examined did not reveal who the actual sender of the message is.

No specific provisions regarding the hierarchical rank of law issued under current circumstances were found in the available Argentine laws sources. It seems probable, however, that given the broad powers granted to the president and the military junta one may find a variety of substances and hierarchical levels assigned to these instruments.

TRATADO INTERNACIONAL (International Treaty). According to the charter, international treaties and agreements are, together with the constitution and the laws enacted in pursuance thereof, the supreme law of the nation.[22] The fundamental text, however, does not provide a hierarchical ranking among these primary sources of law. Nevertheless, a renowned Argentine scholar stated that international agreements are subordinate to the constitution and have a rank equivalent to the ordinary laws.[23]

International treaties and agreements are negotiated to completion by the president of the nation;[24] however, their enforceability requires congressional approval, by passing a law, and by observing the ordinary legislative procedure.[25]

Current Status. According to the Statute for the Process of National Reorganization, the powers granted to the president of the nation by the charter as regards international treaties and agreements remains within his competence.[26] The related powers granted to Congress by the charter have been added to and absorbed by the president under the statute.[27] Consequently, under the current circumstances, the entire process affecting treaties and agreements is totally entrusted to the chief executive. There were no references, statutory or otherwise, to the rank of international instruments.

DECRETO (Decree). The president of the nation is the trustee of the executive power. He performs his functions through decrees which must be issued under the signature of the chief executive and the corresponding minister of the cabinet in order to be enforceable.[28]

Decrees may contain general provisions or may cover specific matters. Whatever the content, all decrees bear the same designation. Those controlling general matters are referred to as *reglamentos* (regulations) and *decretos reglamentarios* (regulatory decrees) and in practice have been assigned a higher rank than that of the ordinary decrees.[29]

All decrees are subordinate to the constitution, the laws, and the treaties with foreign powers.[30] Like all legislative instruments, decrees must be published in the official gazette in order to be enforceable.

It must be kept in mind that some decrees have been issued and probably will continue to be issued covering matters supposedly reserved for the ordinary laws. Although no specific provisions or references were found in the charter or in the related statutes supporting such issuances, this apparently has been a matter of practice. These decrees have been assigned the force of law by enforcement agencies, the courts, and the scholars alike.[31] Some authors referred to them as "decree-laws," others as "decrees of urgent necessity." They are published in the official gazette under the heading decree-law. These decrees are understood to require the subsequent approval of Congress.[32]

Some academicians have referred to the existance of decree-laws proper, but these were found to have been issued, by and large, by de facto governments.[33]

Current Status. The current statutory material governing the functions of the state do not include references to decrees. A perusal of official gazettes revealed that these instruments are being used in exactly the same manner as they were before. There are no indications that decree-laws have been issued by the military junta so far.

Notes

1. H. J. Zarini, *Constitución de la nación argentina, concordada con sus reformas y antecedentes* (Buenos Aires: Editorial Astrea, 1973), art. 31 (hereafter cited as Zarini, *Const.*).
2. Zarini, *Const.*, art. 30; R. Bielsa, *Derecho Constitucional*, 2d ed. (Buenos Aires: R. Depalma, 1954), pp. 81, 82 (hereafter cited as Bielsa, *Derecho*).
3. Bielsa, *Derecho*, pp. 81, 82.
4. *Estatuto para el proceso de reorganización nacional, Boletin Oficial* (*B.O.*) (March 31, 1976) (hereafter cited as *Estatuto*).
5. *Acta para el proceso de reorganización nacional, B.O.* (March 29, 1976).
6. *Estatuto*.
7. Ibid., art. 14.
8. Law 21,256 of March 24, 1976, *B.O.* (March 26, 1976) (hereafter cited as Law 21,256.
9. Zarini, *Const.*, art. 36.
10. Ibid., arts. 68, 69, 72, and 86, no. 4.
11. Ibid., art. 68.
12. Ibid., art. 44.
13. Ibid., arts. 69, 70, and 72.
14. Bielsa, *Derecho*, p. 432.
15. Ibid.
16. Zarini, *Const.*, art. 73.
17. V. Sarsfield, *Código Civil, con notas* (Buenos Aires: Editorial Claridad, 1975), art. 2.
18. Zarini, *Const.*, art. 31.
19. *Estatuto*, art. 5.
20. Ibid., arts. 5 and 8.
21. Law 21,256.
22. Zarini, *Const.*, art. 31.
23. M. S. Marienhoff, *Tratado de derecho administrativo* (Buenos Aires: Abeledo-Perrot, 1965), 1:265,266 (hereafter cited as Marienhoff, *Tratado*).
24. Zarini, *Const.*, art. 67, no. 19.
25. Marienhoff, *Tratado*, p. 263.
26. *Estatuto*, art. 4.
27. Ibid., art. 5.
28. Zarini, *Const.*, art. 87.
29. Bielsa, *Derecho*, p. 537; A. A. Gordillo, *Tratado de derecho administrativo, parte general* (Buenos Aires: Ediciones Macchi, 1974), V: 50, 51 (hereafter cited as Gordillo, *Tratado*).
30. Zarini, *Const.*, art. 31.
31. Gordillo, *Tratado*, V: 38, 39, and 40.
32. Bielsa, *Derecho*, p. 534.
33. Gordillo, *Tratado*, V: 37.

Bolivia

Under the Constitution

1. Constitution
2. Interpretative Laws
3. Law Treaties
4. Supreme Decree

Current Status

1. Constitution Decree Law
2. Supreme Decree

CONSTITUCIÓN (Constitution). According to the Bolivian constitution enacted on February 2, 1967,[1] and brought into effect for the second time by Decree Law 11,947 of November 9, 1974,[2] the charter is the supreme law of the nation. Its provisions shall prevail over any other legislative enactments.[3] This supremacy is reaffirmed by other provisions in the constitution which bar the laws of the nation from altering the charter and instruct both judicial and administrative authorities to apply and enforce the constitution before and above all other laws.[4]

The national charter only allows for partial amendment, to be initiated by the national Congress. Amendments to the constitution require two separate congressional enactments issued in two separate congressional constitutional terms. The first enactment provides a precise and specific reference to the need for the amendment. The corresponding bill may be introduced before either chamber of the legislature, the Senate or the Chamber of Deputies, in the manner prescribed by the charter. If the statement and proposal are approved by Congress, they are then forwarded to the executive branch for promulgation. Apparently no veto power is granted to the executive in this regard. The second enactment provides for the final approval of the proposed amendment. Both legislative actions require the favorable vote of two-thirds of the attending members in each house for approval. The president of the republic promulgates the amendment but may not veto the amendatory bill.[5]

Interpretation of constitutional provisions may only be conducted by a special category of legislative enactments designated *leyes interpretativas* (interpretative laws). These laws are enacted by the legislature and their issuance requires the favorable vote of two-thirds of the attending members. Interpretative laws may not be affected by executive veto.[6]

No references concerning the hierarchical rank of interpretative laws were found in the constitution or in the related statutory and doctrinal sources available. One author who was consulted stated that these laws actually do not constitute new legislation since they only define the meaning of a given constitutional passage already in force.[7]

Current Status. On August 22, 1971, Gen. Hugo Banzer Suárez siezed power in Bolivia and was sworn in as president of the republic by the military high command.

After several attempts at writing a new constitution, General Banzer and his cabinet ministers issued Decree-Law 11,947 on November 9, 1974, containing a new Statute of Government. There is no specific reference to constitutional power in this statute. A careful reading of the preliminary statements may, however, lead one to infer that this power is in fact vested in the executive branch, composed of the president of the republic (who is also captain general of the armed forces of the nation) and the Council of Ministers of the State.[8]

The same statute stated that the Constitution of 1967 remains in force "insofar as it does not oppose the provisions contained in the statute of government that have an institutional character and other provisions issued by the government through decree laws pursuant to the superior interests of the fatherland."[9] It is therefore quite possible that the constitution be contradicted by executive issuances or, more importantly, be expressly amended thereby. All these issuances are made in the form of decree laws which are printed in the national official gazette under the heading Supreme Decrees.

LEY (Law). Under the charter of 1967, the Bolivian Congress consisting of two chambers, the Senate and the Chamber of Deputies,was invested with the legislative power.[10] Nevertheless, the president of the republic was assigned an equally important role in the lawmaking process.[11]

As a general rule, laws may be introduced as bills either in the Senate or in the Chamber of Deputies by one or more of their respective members. The executive branch may also be the proponent of a bill by means of a message.[12] The executive is the exclusive proponent of bills on such matters as taxation, public expenditures, and development plans. The Supreme Court may submit bills concerning judicial matters and amendments to the various codes, also by means of a message.[13]

The congressional legislative process entails debates in both the Senate and the Chamber of Deputies.[14] When these debates lead to a disagreement between the two houses, the charter provides that a joint session shall be held for a resolution.[15] There are specific provisions covering the problem of legislative inaction or failure to proceed within a prescribed period of time.[16]

The constitution further grants the executive the power to veto legislative enactments within ten days.[17] In such cases, the bill is returned to Congress for consideration in a joint session of both chambers. Congress may either accept or reject the executive veto. Congressional decisions must be supported by the favorable vote of at least two-thirds of the membership to overrule the presidential veto.[18]

Laws are promulgated by the president of the republic. He is compelled to do so when he does not veto a bill, when he fails to exercise his veto power within the prescribed term, or when his veto is overruled by congress in accordance with the provisions of the charter. The executive's failure to promulgate under these circumstances empowers the congress's president to do so.[19]

Promulgation of laws is made with an introductory statement, "Whereas the National Congress has sanctioned the following law . . . therefore, I [the president] promulgate it so that it may be upheld and obeyed as law of the republic."[20] Both the text of the law and its promulgation are contained in the same instrument and are published under an assigned sequential number.

Laws are enforceable on the date of their publication unless otherwise instructed in the text of the law concerned.[21] The requirement of publication is complied with through the national official gazette designated *Gaceta Oficial de Bolivia.*

Laws are directly subordinate to the constitution.[22]

Current Status. The Statute of Government cited above makes no specific references to the legislative power. Nevertheless, a perusal of the statute's content only leads to the conclusion that this constitutional prerogative is again vested in the executive branch. This assertion is supported by the instruments published in the official gazette during the last few years which include legislative material formerly entrusted to the action of the legislature. They were found to have the content of the decree laws currently issued by the president of the republic and the Council of Ministers. The interested reader will find them listed in the table of contents of the official gazette under the heading Supreme Decrees. No special or separate serial numbers were found to have been assigned to them. Finally, they may include legislative material as well as administrative provisions.

Decree laws issued by de facto Bolivian governments are often found to have been issued in several different periods in the past, a fact consistently reported by commentators. Some scholars have speculated that these decree laws cease to have effect as soon as a constitutional government assumes power. Nevertheless, they have unanimously agreed that these instruments continue to be enforced regardless of their sources of origin, are upheld by the courts of law, and are implemented until a law is enacted to directly or indirectly repeal them.[23]

DECRETO SUPREMO (Supreme Decree). This is the basic instrument through which the president of the republic performs most of his administrative functions.[24] Even though the constitution makes direct references to this category of executive issuance,[25] no specific provisions were found regarding the formal aspects of their issuance. A number of copies of the national gazette covering the years 1968 to 1969, a period when there was a constitutional government in Bolivia, were examined at random. The findings indicated that at least two types of supreme decrees were issued.

The first and the most numerous were those issued by the Council of Ministers of the State. They invariably carried the signatures of all the ministers of the cabinet in addition to that of the president of the republic. The second type included decrees with no reference to whether they were issued by the Council of Ministers of the State or not. These appeared with the signatures of the president of the republic and the corresponding cabinet minister depending on the matter covered. The constitutional foundation of the supreme decrees is the provision which states, "All decrees and orders of the president of the republic must be countersigned by the appropriate minister of the cabinet. Without this requirement they shall neither be valid nor obeyed."[26]

A perusal of the content of a random number of supreme decrees has not rendered elements sufficient to differentiate the substance or subject matter assigned to each source: the Council of Ministers of the State or the president and one or more cabinet ministers. Supreme decrees of either type have been found to include similar material, general or individual, or legislative or administrative matters without distinction. They all have been assigned to the same serial number sequence. Another confusing observation is that some supreme decrees were found issued by the Council of Ministers of the State; their content bore no noted relationship to many of the signatory ministers' corresponding departments.

Another type of supreme decree found published in the national official gazette and for which there was no apparent constitutional foundation is that issued by the Council of Ministers of the State which is subject to further approval by the legislature. Specialists in the fields of constitutional and administrative law have reported that such decrees have been issued. There is a discrepancy, however, as to the decrees' effectiveness when legislative approval is pending. One author in particular calls them decree laws and believes them to be in force unless they are repealed by the legislature based on a decision rendered by the Supreme Court.[27] Another author states that these decree laws, when issued in case of urgent needs, can have the force and character of a law if and when they are later reaffirmed by the legislature in accordance with the established formalities for the enactment of ordinary bills.[28] He did not refer to the status of an instrument during the interval between the executive issuance and the congressional decision. These decrees take the format of all decrees and are found published in the national official gazette under the heading Supreme Decree.

Current Status. Under the terms of decree law 11,947 the executive power continues to be vested in the president of the republic and the Council of Ministers of the State.[29] The members of the joint command of the national armed forces are also part of the Council of Ministers with the rank of ministers of state. No specific provisions were found in the Statute of Government concerning the procedures to be observed for the performance of the executive functions. Consequently, and according to article 3 of the same statute, the matter should be controlled by the pertinent passages of the constitution itself.[30]

The scanning of hundreds of issues of the official gazette revealed that two types of decrees are included under the heading of Supreme Decrees: presidential decrees and supreme decrees proper. The difference between them depends on whether or not the Council of Ministers was a part of the process. If it was a part, then the resulting instrument is a supreme decree. Presidential decrees are apparently issued as a means to channel such administrative decisions as appointing and dismissing public officials, while supreme decrees may include both administrative as well as legislative provisions. The content of official gazettes further revealed that supreme decrees may be found to repeal decree laws. It was extremely difficult to establish the existence of a consistent pattern for this category of legislative instrument.

TRATADO INTERNACIONAL (International Treaty). Limited and very superficial references were found in Bolivian statutory and legal literary sources concerning the rank of international treaties and agreements. The constitution itself contains only two provisions in this regard which state that among the powers and duties of the president of the republic are to negotiate and conclude treaties with foreign powers, and that approving international treaties is one of the prerogatives of the legislative power.[31]

Nevertheless, an examination of the index to Latin American legislation of the Library of Congress revealed that the most common instrument used to approve an international treaty is the supreme decree. Notwithstanding, there is evidence of the use of such legislative instruments as laws and decree laws. The content in the promulgating instruments of the same category did not seem related.

Current Status. The statements made with regard to the effects of the Statute of Government on the constitution and the law apparently also apply to enactments concerning international treaties and agreements. The absorption of the legislative powers by the executive places the entire process of the negotiation and conclusion of international instruments as well as their approval and promulgation under the responsibility of the executive branch. Scanning the issues of the national official gazette revealed that a vast majority of international treaties and agreements were approved directly through supreme decrees. A small number of treaties was found to have been approved by decree law. Supreme decrees affecting international treaties were issued either with the participation of the Council of Ministers or directly and simply by the president. No consistent patterns in subject matter were detected.

Notes

1. C. F. Trigo, *República de Bolivia, Constitución Política del Estado, con notas*, 12th ed. (La Paz: Gisbert y Cía., 1967) (hereafter cited as Trigo, *Const.*).
2. Decree law no. 11,947 of November 9, 1974, *Gaceta Oficial* (*G.O.*) (November 12, 1974) (hereafter cited as Decree law 11,947).
3. Trigo, *Const.*, art. 228.
4. Ibid., arts. 228 and 229.
5. Ibid., arts. 230 to 232.
6. Ibid., art. 234.
7. R. Canelas López, *Nuevo derecho constitucional boliviano, Socioconstitucionalismo* (La Paz: Editorial Letras, n.d.), p. 38 (hereafter cited as Canelas López, *Nuevo derecho*).
8. Decree law 11,947, art. 9.
9. Ibid., art. 3.
10. Trigo, *Const.*, art. 46.
11. Ibid., arts. 59; 71; 76; and 96, no. 4.
12. Ibid., art. 71.
13. Ibid., art. 71, par. 2.
14. Ibid., arts. 72 and 73.
15. Ibid., art. 74.
16. Ibid., art. 75.
17. Ibid., art. 76.
18. Ibid., art. 77.
19. Ibid., art. 78.
20. Ibid., art. 80.
21. Ibid., art. 81.
22. Ibid., art. 229.
23. J. A. d'Avis S., *Curso de derecho administrativo, doctrina general y legislación boliviana* (La Paz: Editorial Letras, 1960), p. 64; A. Valencia Vega, *Manual de derecho constitucional* (La Paz: Librería Editorial Juventud, 1964), pp. 270, 271 (hereafter cited as Valencia Vega, *Manual*); A. Revilla Quezada, *Curso de derecho administrativo boliviano*, 2d ed. (La Paz: Empresa Industrial Gráfica E. Burillo, 1958), p. 49.
24. Trigo, *Const.*, art. 96, no. 1.
25. Ibid., arts. 96, no. 1; 99; 102; and 111, par. 2.
26. Ibid., art. 102.
27. Canelas López, *Nuevo derecho*, p. 225.
28. Valencia Vega, *Manual*, p. 270.
29. Decree law 11,947, art. 9.
30. Ibid., art. 3.
31. Trigo, *Const.*, arts. 96, no. 2; and 59, no. 12.

BRAZIL

Under the Constitution

1. Constitution
2. Legislative Decree   Complementary Law
3. Ordinary Law   Treaties   Decree Law   Delegated Law
4. Decree

Current Status

1. Institutional Act
2. Complementary Act

CONSTITUIÇÃO (Constitution). The charter in force was enacted by the national Congress on January 24, 1967. The original text, subject to a number of amendments incorporated into it pursuant to Institutional Act no. 16 of October 14, 1969, and Institutional Act no. 5, art. 2, par. 1 of December 13, 1968, entrusted the cabinet ministers for the navy, army, and air force with the task of producing an integrated version of the charter. A new constitutional text was enacted on October 17, 1969, and further amendments were enacted on May 9, 1972, June 15, 1972, April 23, 1975, and June 28, 1975.[1]

Although no provision in the charter expressly states that the constitution is the supreme law of the land, this may be inferred from the content of the following passages:

> If the president of the republic judges the bill, wholly or in part, unconstitutional . . . he shall veto it.[2]

> Only by the vote of an absolute majority of their members may the courts declare a law or an act of the public power unconstitutional.[3]

There are special provisions in the constitution concerning the amendment process. These procedural formalities are more strict than those normally required for the amendment of regular statutes. The charter may only be amended by at least one-third of the membership of either the Chamber of Deputies or the federal Senate, or by the president of the republic.[4] Two sessions of the national Congress, taking place within sixty days of the presentation of the proposal[5] are required to debate the proposal and vote on it. Only when the two sessions of each of the House and the Senate approve the proposal by two-thirds majority will such approval be valid.

Amendments to the charter shall be promulgated by the superior officers in the Chamber of Deputies and the federal Senate, who are the president, vice-president, and secretary of each of the two houses.[6] Amendments appear in the constitution under the heading *emenda* in sequential numbers.[7]

ATO INSTITUCIONAL (Institutional Act). This instrument has no apparent legal origin or foundation except the self-generating power seized by peoples or groups under certain circumstances. In the case of Brazil, there are different bodies responsible for the issuance of institutional acts. Seventeen of these legislative instruments have been issued so far: one by the supreme command of the revolution, represented by the commanders in chief of the army, navy, and air force; ten by the president of the republic supported by the signature of a number of cabinet ministers; and six by the government of the revolution represented by the cabinet ministers of the navy, army, and air force.[8]

All of the acts carried provisions related to the constitution. They were used either to reenforce a previous charter, enforce a new charter, or amend an existing one. However, reference to these constitutional effects may or may not be expressly stated.

The Constitution of 1967 as amended provided that institutional act no. 5 of December 13, 1968, and others issued thereafter shall continue in force.[9] Consequently, there are about thirteen institutional acts still in force at the time of this writing.[10] Considering their subject matter, origin, and actual ranking within the legislative system, institutional acts are indeed constitutional provisions coexisting with the charter despite their peculiar nature. The president is empowered to repeal the acts when their partial or total content are deemed no longer necessary provided that the opinion of the National Security Council has been heard.[11] It is not clear whether or not the Brazilian executive branch currently has the power to issue further institutional acts. A study of sources available in the Library of Congress reveals that there have been no more such instruments since the enactment of amendment no. 1. The constitution was amended four times since then, each time in accordance with the corresponding provision of the charter itself. In view of the fact that the preliminary statements of the institutional acts repeatedly assigned the constituent power to the president of the republic in his capacity as a head of the revolutionary movement and supreme commander of the armed forces, the possibility of further issuances of these instruments should not be ruled out.

ATO COMPLEMENTAR (Complementary Act). This instrument is issued by the president of the republic by virtue of a number of specific delegations of power vested in him under the provisions of various institutional acts. For example, one act granted the president of the republic the power to suspend the national congress, the legislative assemblies and other high legislative bodies at either federal or state levels and to assume their respective powers.[12] The specific suspension of a given body is, therefore, effected by a complementary act. Likewise, the president may suspend any citizen's political rights for ten years through the same instrument and terminate the mandate of any elected federal congressmen.

No specific references were found in the sources consulted regarding the rank of this instrument within the legal system; however, if the content of the institutional acts is considered, it may be proposed that there is an apparent subordination of the complementary act to the institutional act since the latter granted the president of the republic, explicitly or implicitly, the power to issue complementary acts to implement them.

Concerning the rest of the instruments within the system, no relationship of subordination was evident between the complementary acts and any other legislative instrument, except the institutional acts as stated above. This is apparently reaffirmed by the provision made in almost all institutional acts by which any judicial review of acts performed in pursuance of an institutional act and the resulting complementary acts and effects thereof are excluded.

Finally, as a number of institutional acts are still in force, the president of the republic continues to have the power to issue complementary acts. In fact, a quick review of recent issues of the *Diario Oficial* revealed that some still may be found.

LEI COMPLEMENTAR (Complementary or Supplementary Law). Enactment of this instrument is entrusted by the constitution to the legislative power, which is vested in the federal Congress consisting of a Chamber of Deputies and a Senate.[13] The pertinent passage in the charter is not very clear about the circumstances or categories for which a complementary law should be enacted. The ranking authority of the instrument is not well established either.

A number of legal scholars[14] are inclined to believe that this legislative instrument should only be enacted when the constitution specifically requires so. Their argument is that the special nature of this law is established by the fact that stricter requirements are to be met for its enactment. In fact, they add, there are several provisions in the constitution stating that certain matters should be controlled only by this type of legislative enactment, e.g., establishment of a new state and territorial divisions, permission for foreign armed forces to pass through or remain in the territory, and taxation.

Concerning the legislative process, the charter provides that the complementary law shall be enacted only if it obtains majority of the votes of the members of each house and the other standards of voting provided for ordinary laws are observed.[15]

No reference was found in the constitution to the participation of the president of the republic either in the sanctioning or the vetoing of this legal instrument. There is disagreement among Brazilian authors in this regard.[16] Some scholars believe that complementary laws should be approved by the president. Reportedly, constitutional practices reveal that the president does in fact participate in these laws in the same manner prescribed for the promulgation of ordinary laws.[17]

According to a Brazilian legal scholar, the complementary law belongs to a third gender of ranking within the legal system. It is placed between the ordinary law and the constitution as well as the amendments thereof. Consequently, a complementary law may not contradict the constitution; but ordinary statutes, decree laws, and the delegated law must all conform to complementary laws.[18]

TRATADO INTERNACIONAL (International Treaty). According to the charter, the state has the power to maintain relations with foreign nations and negotiate treaties and conventions with them.[19] The exercise of this power is vested in the president of the republic who is entrusted with concluding international treaties, conventions, and related acts, subject to the approval of the Brazilian national Congress.[20]

The charter further provides that it is the Congress which has the exclusive power "to render final decision regarding international treaties, agreements and related acts concluded by the president of the republic. . . ."[21] The instrument by means of which this congressional approval is granted is a *decreto legislativo*, or legislative decree.

There are no apparent specific provisions concerning the effects that treaties and agreements may have on other legislative instruments. Nevertheless, other constitutional provisions suggest that they are at least equivalent to the ordinary statute. One example of this apparent equivalency may be found in the provision by which the federal Supreme Court is given competence to hear and decide on appeal cases denying enforcement of a federal treaty or an ordinary statute and to declare an international treaty or a statute unconstitutional.[22]

The above assertion has been supported by a scholar who stated that under Brazilian law international treaties and agreements can only be perfected with the approval of the national Congress because of their relevance and national consequences, and more importantly, because they frequently require amending the laws of the land.[23]

LEI (Law). This is the most typical legal instrument which is issued by the legislative power when there is no other particular instrument required by the constitution. Even though the constitution explicitly refers to it as ordinary law, it is not published under that title. No specific references have been found to the content of the law. Although laws usually concern substantive matters or procedural precepts, more often than not they cover such administrative considerations as naming a museum, granting pensions to widows, and authorizing credit operations.

Bills may be introduced by an individual member or committee of either the Chamber of Deputies or the Senate, by the president of the republic, or by a federal court having jurisdiction throughout the national territory.[24] The presidential initiative becomes exclusive on finances, the strength of the armed forces, the civil service, and other matters expressly enumerated by the charter.[25] Federal courts may only introduce bills on the creation, termination, and salaries of judicial positions.[26]

By and large, debates on bills introduced may be initiated in either the Chamber of Deputies or the Senate. Those introduced by the president are first assigned to the Chamber of Deputies except when the president alleges urgency. In the latter case the bill is submitted to a joint session of the national Congress.[27] Ordinarily bills are debated and voted upon in both the Chamber of Deputies and the Senate. The charter provides a number of procedural rules to be observed within the two bodies and between them when transferring the bill for consideration from one to the other. Additional norms control the bill's remission to the president for his sanction or veto.[28] The president may do the latter wholly or in part, on grounds of unconstitutionality or of being contrary to the public interest. If the term for vetoing expires without the president acting on it, the bill shall be considered legally approved.[29]

Vetoes are considered by the national Congress in joint sessions. A favorable two-thirds vote in each legislative body is required to overrule the president.[30] An interesting feature of the Brazilian veto is that in cases of partial veto only the vetoed portion of the bill returns to Congress; the remainder of the bill is sanctioned and promulgated as is. If the vetoed portion is later approved, it is promulgated as an entirely separate law with a different number. Enforcement of each portion may, and often does, start on different dates.[31]

Ordinarily promulgation of the laws is made by the president of the republic. Should he fail to do so in due time, the president of the federal Senate shall proceed accordingly.[32] Publication of the law in the *Diario Oficial* is controlled by a regulatory statute which includes the time within which the law shall take effect.[33]

LEI DELEGADA (Delegated Law). This is a legislative instrument drafted and sometimes sanctioned by a body other than the legislature. Under the Brazilian constitution, this procedure may take place when the national Congress delegates its legislative enacting power on certain matters which are not of its exclusive competence for a limited period of time to the president of the republic, a committee of either the House or the Senate, or Congress itself.[34] This delegation is made by means of a congressional resolution which shall specifically define the subject matter and the period of time during which it shall be validly exercised.[35]

In the case of congressional delegation of legislative powers to the president of the republic and within the terms of this delegation, the president is free to act on one or more instruments at his own discretion. Delegations to the president may be granted in two forms: with subsequent congressional approval of the enactment or without approval.[36]

When the delegation requires congressional approval, the president drafts the bill, sanctions it, and submits it to Congress which acts on the bill in a single voting session. Under the charter, Congress may not introduce any amendments; it can only approve or reject.[37] When congressional approval is not required, the entire processing of the law rests with the president, who drafts, sanctions, promulgates, and publishes the delegated law without any intervention from the legislature.[38]

Despite the apparent simplicity of the constitutional passages, legal scholars disagree on the interpretation of the constitutional provision. Some of them propose that under no circumstance could congressional delegation of legislative power to the president mean that final congressional approval is not required even if the text of the congressional resolution does not include this requirement.

Delegation of legislative power to a congressional committee may or may not require further approval.[39] The standard procedure in these cases is to publish the instrument before it is sent to the president for sanctioning and promulgation. This allows the majority of the committee members, or one-fifth of either the House or the Senate, to request that the committee's issuances be subject to joint approval of both the House and Senate.[40] Further regulation regarding this instrument may be found in the rules of Congress.

The hierarchy of this legislative instrument is at the same level as the ordinary law.

DECRETO-LEI (Decree Law). The Brazilian charter provides that the president of the republic may, in cases of urgency or important public interest and when no increase in expenditures will result, issue decree laws on the following matters: national security, public finance, including standards on taxation, and the establishment of positions and salaries for the civil service. Decree laws do not require a congressional delegation of power. The president drafts, sanctions, promulgates, and publishes the bill by himself. No further action is required for its enforceability. Nevertheless, Congress may act upon it within a period of sixty days from its promulgation either affirming or rejecting, but may not introduce amendments. If there is no congressional action within the stipulated period the text is final and considered to have the endorsement of the legislature.[41]

Examination of a number of issues of the *Diario Oficial* revealed that approval of legislative decrees is achieved by a legislative decree which only cites the instrument and expresses approval of the corresponding text.

The constitution further provides that subsequent congressional rejection of a decree law shall not have nullifying effects retroactive to the time of the instrument's date of enforcement.[42] Decree laws share the same level of hierarchy with the ordinary laws and therefore may or may not have either derogatory or amendatory effects thereon.

DECRETO LEGISLATIVO (Legislative Decree). According to a Brazilian scholar the legislative decree is the means by which the national Congress exercises its exclusive powers. The procedural steps followed for the enactment of this instrument are the same as those observed for the enactment of the regular law with the important exception that the participation of the president of the republic is not required for either sanctioning or promulgating.[43] According to the charter, legislative decrees shall be promulgated by the president of the federal state and are published in the *Diario Oficial.*[44] This instrument is only subordinate in authority to the constitution. Since constitutional matters are the exclusive subjects for the legislative decree, it seems unlikely that this instrument could interfere with the law and related regulatory statutes.

DECRETO (Decree). The Brazilian constitution prescribes that the president of the republic is entrusted with the exclusive power to issue decrees and regulations for the faithful implementation of the laws.[45] This instrument is therefore subordinate to the regular laws or statutes and may or may not contain particular or general provisions.[46] Since the decree is a presidential act, it must also be countersigned by the corresponding minister of the cabinet.[47] The constitution also provides that the president's power to issue decrees may be delegated by him to his cabinet ministers.[48] This instrument is also published in the *Diario Oficial.*

Notes

1. *Constituição federal e constituições estaduais,* vol. 1 (Senado Federal: Subsecretaria de Edições Técnicas, 1975) (hereafter cited as *Const.*); for an English version see *Constitution of Brazil, 1967, as Amended by Constitutional Amendment No. 1 of October 17, 1969* (Washington, D.C.: Organization of American States, 1970).

2. Ibid., art. 59, par. 1.

3. Ibid., art. 116.

4. Ibid., art. 47.

5. Ibid., art. 48.

6. As observed in the text published in the *Diario Oficial.*

7. *Const.*, art. 49.

8. *Emendas constitucionais 1 a 3, atos institucionais 1 a 17, atos complementares 1 a 96, leis complementares 1 a 12; Legislação citada, sinopse* (Brasilia, 1972) (hereafter cited as *Emendas*).

9. *Const.*, art. 182.

10. April 1, 1977.

11. *Const.*, art. 182, sole par.

12. *Ato Institucional, no. 5, art. 2, Emendas.*

13. *Const.*, art. 27.

14. M. G. Ferreira, *Curso de direito constitucional* (São Paulo: Saraiva, 1967), p. 214 (hereafter cited as Ferreira, *Curso*).

15. *Const.*, art. 50.

16. Pontes de Miranda, *Comentários à constituição de 1967, con a emenda no. 1 de 1969,* 2d ed. (São Paulo: Revista dos Tribunais, 1970), 3: 140 (hereafter cited as Miranda, *Comentários*); Ferreira, *Curso,* p. 215.

17. Ferreira, *Curso,* p. 215.

18. Ibid., p. 213.

19. *Const.*, art. 8, par. I.

20. Ibid., art. 81, par. X.

21. Ibid., art. 44, par. I.

22. Ibid., art. 119, par. III a and b.

23. M. G. Ferreira, *Comentários à constituição brasileira, emenda constitucional no. 1 de 17 de outubro de 1969* (São Paulo: Saraiva, 1974), 2: 140 (hereafter cited as Ferreira, *Comentários*).

24. *Const.*, art. 56.

25. Ibid., arts. 57 and 109.

26. Ibid., art. 115, par. II.

27. Ibid., arts. 56, sole par., and 51, par. 2.

28. Ibid., arts. 57, 58, and 59.

29. Ibid., art. 59, pars. 1 and 2.

30. Ibid., art. 59, par. 3.

31. Ferreira, *Curso,* p. 194.

32. *Const.*, art. 59, pars. 3, 4, and 5.

33. Decree law 4657 of September 4, 1942, *Código Civil Brasileiro,* 26th ed. (Rio de Janeiro: Saraiva, 1976).

34. *Const.*, art. 52.

35. Ibid.

36. Ferreira, *Curso,* p. 203.

37. *Const.*, art. 54, sole par.

38. Ferreira, *Curso,* p. 203.

39. Ibid., p. 205.

40. *Const.*, art. 53.

41. *Const.*, art. 55, par. 1.

42. Ibid., art. 55, par. 2.

43. Miranda, *Comentários,* p. 142; Ferreira, *Comentários* 1 (1972): 268.

44. *Const.*, art. 59.

45. Ibid., art. 81, par. III.

46. L. P. Ferreira, *Curso de direito constitucional,* 2d ed. (Recife: Co. Editôra de Pernambuco, 1970), p. 344.

47. *Const.*, art. 85, par. I.

48. Ibid., art. 85, par. IV.

chile

Under the Constitution

1. Constitution

2. Law   Decree with Force of Law   Treaties

3. Regulatory Decree

4. Decree

Current Status

1. Constitution   Constitutional Act (Decree Law)

2. Decree Law   Treaties

3. Decree

CONSTITUCION (Constitution). The Chilean charter presently in force was enacted in 1925 after it was submitted to a plebiscite.[1] The original text was amended several times. Although there is no specific provision in the constitution stating that the charter is supreme over all other legislative instruments, its rank is determined by a number of articles the most relevant of which establishes the constitutional tribunal. The tribunal's main purpose is to ascertain and decide upon the constitutionality of the bills and international treaties submitted to the legislature for consideration and action and of the decree laws issued by the president of the republic. The supremacy of the constitution is further reaffirmed by the special procedure prescribing its amendment.[2] Broadly speaking, the amendments to the constitution go through the same procedural steps as the laws with the additional requirements that a higher proportion of votes is needed to approve the amendment and that both the Chamber of Deputies and the Senate, acting as a whole body, participate in a later stage of the procedure. Furthermore, the citizenry may partake of the amendatory process in a plebiscite.[3]

The physical format of a constitutional amendment is that of a law or *ley* which, when promulgated, simply falls under the sequential number assigned to this category of legislative instruments and, of course, is published in the *Diario Oficial.* Once the amendment is enacted its content is integrated into the text of the charter and assumes the corresponding rank.[4]

Current Status. On September 11, 1973, the commanders in chief of the army, navy, and air force, and the police seized power in Chile and constituted a *junta de gobierno* to rule the country. According to the junta's first legislative act, the constitution remained in force "to the extent possible under the present circumstances. . . ."[5] Within the same calendar year, the national Congress was dissolved by another decree law issued by the junta.[6]

On June 26, 1974, and again by decree law, the junta vested itself with the constituent power provided to be exercised by means of decree laws signed by all its members[7] and formalized its assumption of all government powers by vesting itself with legislative prerogatives. The basic legislative function was also exercised through decree laws. It was thought that this situation could lead to considerable confusion because of the concentration of two fundamental functions through only one instrument. Thus provisions carrying constitutional repercussions as well as those of a mere legislative content were issued in similar formats and therefore are difficult to identify. To solve the problem a decree law was issued providing that all previous decree laws opposing the constitution should be treated as constitutional amendments, and that from that date on decree laws issued under the constituent power should explicitly state so.[8] Consequently decree laws issued thereafter had to bear the title *acta constitutional* (constitutional act) immediately under the heading *Decreto ley* (Decree law). The heading was numbered with the regular serial, and the title was given another separate number. It was also provided that within the term of one year decree laws which have amended the constitution in connection with the powers of the state and their exercise shall take the form of a constitutional act.[9] Nevertheless, amendments to the acts introduced by means of decree laws have carried neither the title nor the number of the former.

No difference was noted regarding the procedure set forth by the junta for the performance of these supposedly separate functions.[10]

As to the authority rank of the act, it shares the level of the constitution. All constitutional acts issued up to now have amended or repealed many precepts of the constitution. Acts are published in the *Diario Oficial.*

LEY (Law). According to the national charter, the law is the instrument enacted with the participation of both the national Congress and the president of the republic by the procedure set forth in the constitution. There are no provisions confining the legislative power to any specific branch of the government.[11]

A law may be introduced as a bill by any member of the House or Senate, or by the president of the republic. There are some specific exemptions by which the legislative initiative is vested exclusively in the president of the republic who introduces the bill on these matters by means of a "message."[12]

The general rule is that bills for a law are introduced in either the House or the Senate. Such areas of legislative concern as taxation, budget, and induction into the armed forces may only be introduced in the Chamber of Deputies or House. Bills on amnesty and general pardons may only be introduced in the Senate.[13] Even though the general rule is that bills are debated and voted upon separately in the House and in the Senate,[14] the constitution provides that when agreement between the two bodies has not been reached on fundamental points, a joint committee may be established to take action. Joint action also occurs when the relevance or complexity of a given bill requires a joint effort. Regular legislative committees may also deliberate and vote on certain bills under special circumstances.[15]

Bills favorably decided upon by both the House and Senate are submitted to the president of the republic who may concur and promulgate or veto.[16] If the president does not act within the term established by the constitution, the bill automatically becomes law and can be enforced after promulgation.[17] If the president vetoes the bill, it returns to Congress with the objections appended for consideration of both the House and the Senate in separate sessions. Congress can override the presidential veto by insisting on a favorable vote supported by two-thirds of the attending members of each legislative body.[18]

Bills that are approved by both Congress and the president are promulgated by the latter by means of a *decreto* (decree).[19] When a bill has not been promulgated by the president within the prescribed term, or when the content of the bill is altered for promulgation, the constitutional tribunal, by congressional request, may promulgate the law by means of a *fallo* (decision).[20] Laws promulgated by either the president or the constitutional tribunal are published in the *Diario Oficial.* Laws are subordinate only to the constitution.

Current Status. As stated in the preceding section on the constitution, the *junta de gobierno* vested itself with the legislative power through decree laws.[21] Decisions by the junta are made by unanimous vote. The junta further regulated its legislative functions and established four committees to provide it with legislative assistance. Functions previously assigned to Congress by the constitution were transferred to these committees by the junta through a decree which also provided for procedural steps to be followed for the enactment of decree laws.[22] The preceding provisions were further regulated by decree.[23] These decree laws are promulgated by the president of the republic and must be published in the *Diario Oficial.*

TRATADO INTERNACIONAL (International Treaty). Pursuant to the constitution, international treaties are negotiated by the president of the republic but must be approved by the national Congress before presidential ratification.[24] The procedural steps followed to enact an international treaty as the law of the land are the same as for the regular statute, or *ley*, except that there is no presidential veto. Congressional approval of an international treaty is given in the form of an *acuerdo* (agreement). The ensuing presidential ratification is performed through a simple decree which technically promulgates the treaty which becomes enforceable after publication in the *Diario Oficial.*

The constitution does not assign any given rank to international treaties. Scholars consider these instruments as strong as regular statutes or laws.[25] Apparently conflict between a regular national statute and a promulgated international treaty has not been given enough attention in Chilean legal literature. Only one available source was found which addressed itself to the point by stating that regular national statutes may derogate international treaties by limiting or altogether barring their international enforcement.[26]

Current Status. Under the present circumstances, a decree law has provided that international treaties shall be signed by the minister of foreign affairs as an authorized plenipotentiary. Then the instrument is submitted to the *junta de gobierno* which may approve or reject the treaty. If the instrument is approved, the junta expresses itself through a decree law. Ratification is performed by the president of the junta and the minister of foreign affairs. Finally the instrument is promulgated by a *decreto-supremo* (supreme decree) issued by the minister of foreign affairs and published in the *Diario Oficial* for its enforcement.[27]

DECRETO CON FUERZA DE LEY (Decree with Force of Law). The constitution provides that the legislative power may authorize the president of the republic to issue decrees with the force of law on certain subjects indicated therein, including such administrative matters as government organization and civil service. This congressional authorization may only be granted for a limited period of time and shall specify the matters to be covered as well as any limitations, restrictions, and formalities to be observed. Decrees with force of law are supposed to be equivalent to a law except that their content shall always conform to the law which authorized their issuance.[28] Since they carry statutory force, decrees with force of law must be published in the *Diario Oficial.*[29]

Each series of authorized issuances is assigned a numbering sequence starting with one and includes the signature of the president of the republic and the corresponding minister or ministers of his cabinet.

DECRETO (Decree). This instrument is sometimes designated as *decreto supremo* (supreme decree) and is the means by which the president of the republic exercises his administrative and related governmental functions.[30]

As a general rule decrees are signed by the president of the republic and the corresponding minister or ministers of the cabinet, which is a legal requirement for the validation or enforceability of the decree.[31] Some decrees, however, may be found published with only the signature of the corresponding minister or ministers of the cabinet. In this case, there is always a statement by the signatory cabinet member reading *por orden del Presidente de la República* (by instruction of the president of the republic).

There are cases where decrees are objected to by the *Contraloría General de la República,* an independent official agency entrusted with the power to control the legality of these instruments in their formal and substantive aspects. Under these circumstances, the president may insist on the issuance of the decree concerned and command, by a second decree, the *contraloría* to register the first decree provided his insistence is supported by the signatures of all the ministers of the cabinet. The second decree is known as the *decreto de insistencia.*[32] The same kind of total cabinet support is required by the law when the president, under circumstances of public calamity, foreign aggression, or others provided for by the constitution, issues decrees ordering expenditures authorized by the law.[33]

Other agencies may also issue decrees. In Spanish these instruments are called *decreto* but are never referred to as *decreto supremo,* a designation reserved only for presidential decrees.

Concerning rank of authority, there are two kinds of decrees, *decreto reglamentario* (regulatory decree) and *decreto simple* (simple decree). The first category may sometimes be found published under the heading *decreto* with the word *reglamento* or *reglamento de . . .* immediately below it on the second line. A regulatory decree consists of general norms while that of the simple decree is of a singular or individual nature, such as granting to a specific individual or corporation the benefit or benefits legally available to them. While regulatory decrees are subordinate to the law and the constitution,[34] the simple decree is subordinate to the regulatory decree and to all other higher instruments.[35]

Current Status. The executive power is now vested in the president of the *junta de gobierno*[36] who exercises his functions as does the previously described president of the republic. The instruments he issues correspond, broadly speaking, to those issued before September 1973.

DECRETO-LEY (Decree Law). Traditionally there was no constitutional foundation for this category of instrument which has been established by de facto governments when the constitutional process has been interrupted in Chile. They are published under the signature of the de facto president of the republic, or whatever name is given to the chief executive, and the corresponding cabinet minister or ministers. They have been traditionally enforced by the Chilean judiciary and have, consequently, been integrated into the regular system of the country. Reportedly these decree laws have shared the rank of the law.[37] The military junta has now established the legal foundation for this instrument.[38]

Notes

1. F. Cumplido C. and C. Medina Q., *Constitución política de la República de Chile, texto al día, agosto de 1971*, (Santiago: Ed. Universitaria, 1972) (hereafter cited as Cumplido and Medina, *Const.*).
2. Ibid., art. 78-b, sect. a and b.
3. Ibid., arts. 108 and 109.
4. Ibid., art. 110.
5. Decree law 1 of September 11,1973, *Diario Oficial* (*D.O.*) (September 18, 1973), art. 3.
6. Decree law 27 of September 21,1973, *D.O.* (September 24, 1973).
7. Decree law 527 of June 17, 1974, *D.O.* (June 26, 1974), art. 4 (hereafter cited as Decree law 527).
8. Decree law 788 of December 2, 1974, *D.O.* (December 4, 1974).
9. Decree law 1552 of September 11, 1976, *D.O.*, no. 29,558-A (September 13, 1976).
10. Decree law 991 of April 17, 1975, *D.O.* (January 3, 1976) (hereafter cited as Decree law 991).
11. Cumplido and Medina, *Const.*, arts. 45-55; *Código Civil*, official ed. of May 31 (Editorial Jurídica de Chile, 1966), art. 1.
12. Ibid., arts. 44, nos. 4 and 12; 45, and 72, no. 15.
13. Ibid., art. 45.
14. Ibid., arts. 48, 49, and 50.
15. Ibid., art. 51.
16. Ibid., arts. 52 and 53.
17. Ibid., art. 55.
18. Ibid., art. 54.
19. Ibid., arts. 52, 54, 55, and 72, 1.
20. Ibid., art. 78, b.
21. Decree law 527.
22. Decree law 991.
23. Decree 220 of January 30, 1976, *D.O.* (June 21, 1976).
24. Cumplido and Medina, *Const.*, arts. 43, no. 5; and 72, no. 16.
25. A. Silva Bascuñan, *Tratado de derecho constitucional* (Santiago: Editorial Jurídica de Chile, 1963), 3:376-77 (hereafter cited as Silva Bascuñan, *Tratado*); E. Silva Cimma, *Derecho administrativo chileno y comparado*, 3rd ed. (Santiago: Editorial Jurídica de Chile, 1954), 1:167 (hereafter cited as Silva Cimma, *Derecho*).
26. F. Albónico Valenzuela, *Manual de derecho internacional privado* (Santiago: Editorial Jurídica de Chile, 1950), 1:37-38.
27. Decree law 247 of December 3, 1973, *D.O.* (January 17, 1974).
28. Cumplido and Medina, *Const.*, art. 44, no. 15.
29. Ibid.
30. Ibid., arts. 60, 71, and 72.
31. Ibid., art. 75.
32. Law 10,336 of May 29, 1952, art. 13; Silva Cimma, *Derecho*, p. 175.
33. Cumplido and Medina, *Const.*, art. 72, no. 10.

34. Silva Cimma, *Derecho*, p. 234; Silva Bascuñan, *Tratado*, p. 268.
35. Silva Cimma, *Derecho*, pp. 217 and 218.
36. Decree law 527, as amended by Decree law 806 of December 16, 1974, *D.O.* (December 17, 1974).
37. Silva Cimma, *Derecho*, pp. 205 and 206.
38. Decree law 527.

COLUMBIA

1. Constitution

2. Treaties

3. Frame Law   Organic Law

4. Constitutional or Autonomous Regulation   Decree with Force of Law   Ordinary Law

   Extraordinary Decree   Legislative Decree

5. Decree

CONSTITUCIÓN (Constitution). The constitution currently in force was enacted in 1886. It was amended several times, most recently by Legislative Act No. 1 of December 18, 1975.[1] The supremacy of the constitution over all other forms of legislation stems from the provision stating that "in every case of incompatibility between the Constitution and the law, the constitutional provisions shall be applied."[2]

Consistent with the above, the charter also provided for special procedural norms to be followed for its own amendment. The resulting amendatory instrument is enacted under the heading of *Acto Legislativo* (legislative act). The pertinent constitutional passage concerning amendments to the charter states that the constitution may only be amended by a legislative act, which is discussed and approved by Congress at its regular sessions and then published by the government for its final consideration in the ensuing regular legislative period. This consideration consists of a new discussion for final approval by an absolute majority of the members of the House and the Senate. No commentaries have been found on this subject, but examination of the related consititutional passages indicates that only a simple majority is required for the first congressional approval. If the executive branch does not publish the legislative act in due course, the president of the Congress shall do so.[3]

There are special constitutional amendatory provisions concerning the staggering and parity of the liberal and conservative political parties in the branches of the government.[4]

No specific provisions have been found in the constitution concerning the promulgation of the legislative act. The only formality provided for consists of the publication of the instrument in the *Diario Oficial* which, according to statute, is the promulgation itself.[5]

TRATADO INTERNACIONAL (International Treaty). According to the constitution, it is in the power of the president of the republic "to direct diplomatic and commercial relations with other states and entities recognized under international law . . . , to conclude treaties and conventions with other states . . . to be submitted to Congress for approval."[6] The charter further provides that Congress is entrusted with the power to either approve or reject international treaties and conventions entered into with other states or entities under the rules of international law. This power is to be exercised by means of a *ley* (law).[7]

There are no provisions in the charter assigning specific rank to the international treaties and agreements or conventions.

Referring to amendments to an international treaty, a Colombian legal scholar stated that, as a bilateral instrument entered into by sovereign powers, a treaty may not be amended unilaterally. After an international treaty has received congressional approval, its content is incorporated into the national legislation. Only the government may amend it or alter its effects by internationally accepted norms or practices.[8] A June 13, 1925, decision of the Colombian Supreme Court has further stated that Colombian public law consists not only of the constitution and the law but of international treaties with foreign powers which have been signed and properly ratified. It is a principle of public law, according to the Supreme Court of Justice of Colombia, that the constitution and treaties with foreign powers are the supreme law of the land, and their provisions prevail over those of ordinary statutes in cases of conflict.[9] It appears then that international treaties are ranked above the ordinary laws in Colombia.

LEY (Law). This denomination is assigned in Colombia to an instrument enacted by the legislature with the observance of specific procedural steps prescribed by the constitution.[10] The pertinent passages provide that Congress, consisting of a Senate and a House of Representatives,[11] has the power to make laws.[12] The lawmaking process is not confined to Congress; it is shared with the executive branch. Bills may be submitted by either a member of Congress or a minister of the cabinet.[13] Bills concerning such specific matters as the national budget are exclusively the initiative of the executive.[14] The Council of State, a high advisory board of the government, drafts the bills and codes to be submitted for congressional consideration.[15] In practice the council does not submit its drafts directly to Congress. According to a leading scholar in this field, the act of submitting bills to Congress is limited to the members of the cabinet when so prescribed by the charter.[16]

A bill may be submitted to either the House or the Senate for assignment to the corresponding permanent congressional committee for preliminary discussions.[17] Nevertheless, discussions on a bill may not take place until after it has been published as a draft for the congressional agenda.[18]

According to the charter, a bill requires the approval of both legislative bodies before being forwarded to the president of the republic for his approval or rejection.[19] If there is no presidential action on the bill within the prescribed term, the president is then compelled by the constitution to promulgate it into a law, as if he had approved it.[20] If he rejects the bill, it is returned to Congress for consideration by each legislative body.[21] If the term for presidential action is still running but the congressional term is over, the bill is published by the president regardless of his approval or disapproval.[22] Readers may find these unfinished, and therefore unenforceable, statutes printed in the *Diario Oficial.* Presidential vetoes may be overridden in Congress by an absolute majority vote of each of its bodies, except in some cases in which a two-thirds vote is required.[23] When the objection to the bill is on grounds of unconstitutionality, the bill insisted upon by Congress is sent to the Supreme Court of Justice for a decision on the grounds alleged by the executive. If the court upholds the bill as passed by Congress, the president is bound to sanction and promulgate it into law. If the veto prevails, the bill is simply filed away.[24]

The legislative routine requires that promulgation be made by the president of the repulic. Should he fail to do so, the sanctioning and promulgation shall be performed by the president of the Congress who shall also order the corresponding publication in the *Diario Oficial.*[25]

The title of the law must correspond exactly to the content of the bill; its enacting clause shall begin with "the Congress of Colombia decrees . . . ." A new statute becomes enforceable two months after publication.[26]

In addition to ordinary statutes, Colombia has had two types of bills since 1968 which differ from statutes in both procedural steps and legal effects. The first type has been created to redistribute the competence between the president of the republic and the Congress on economics, fiscal, and administrative matters. In these areas of concern, the legislature shall only provide general guidelines.[27] The bills shall be submitted by the president of the republic, and the decrees he issues pursuant to these laws may not be affected by subsequent statutes except when these laws are of the same nature.[28] Legal authors and scholars who participated in the drafting of the 1968 amendment have called these laws *leyes cuadros,* literally frame laws. The other type, known as *leyes orgánicas* or organic laws, is related to the national budget, plans and programs for economic and social development, and public works at the national, provincial, and municipal levels.[29] They are also submitted by the president of the republic. For some of the preceding cases, a different procedure has been prescribed which may determine that the bill be promulgated as a decree with the force of law.[30] These instruments have been assigned a rank higher than the other laws related thereto. Both of these laws are similar in format and are subject to the same publication requirement as is prescribed for ordinary statutes.

DECRETO (Decree). The decree is the typical instrument used by the president of the republic for performing his various functions. Even though the format may be that of the decree, the consequences in terms of rank and legal effects may be different depending on the circumstances.

As a general rule, the president has the power to regulate the ordinary statutes or laws through decrees. They rank directly under the law which in turn must conform to the constitution. Consequently no decree may amend or repeal a law. In case of conflict between the two, the latter shall prevail.[31]

In some specific areas, the president has been granted the power to enact norms on matters not previously regulated by a law, such as a direct legislative function.[32] Reportedly the president acts in such a capacity through a decree, which carries the enforcement strength of an ordinary law and is only subordinate to the constitution; no congressional interference is permitted under the constitution.[33] The executive may be empowered by congressional authorization to enter into contracts, negotiate loans, transfer national property, and exercise other functions within the limits of the constitution such as being temporarily vested with extraordinary powers to meet demands determined by necessity or the public welfare.[34] Under these circumstances, the decrees issued by the president have the force of law. This is a delegated power granted by the principal source, the legislature, directly to the president. As a result, these decrees may only be amended by a law or by other decrees issued under the same congressional delegation of power.[35]

Neither the literature on the topic nor a random sample of issues of the *Diario Oficial* has provided sufficient information to clear up the relative confusion generated by the differing Spanish names assigned to decrees. By and large, they appear under the heading *Decreto* in the official gazette; however, when referred to by other legislative instruments such as laws and decrees, they are called *decretos extraordinarios* (extraordinary decrees). Furthermore, some scholars refer to them as *decreto-leyes* (decree laws);[36] and the constitution simply calls them *decretos* (decrees).[37] It is important that the interested reader keep these formal inconsistencies in mind when working with Colombian sources.

Under the provisions of the constitution, Congress, in the exercise of its legislative powers, may enact laws concerning plans and programs for economic and social development and public works and their funding.[38] A special procedure is required for their enactment,[39] one being that there is a term within which each legislative body should consider and vote on the bill concerned. If this term expires without legislative action, the president may significantly convert the bill into a decree with force of law and promulgate the instrument at his own initiative. Decrees in this category may be assigned a rank equivalent to the ordinary statute.[40] It may be concluded that, within the context of the constitution, these decrees with force of law may only be amended by another law or a decree issued under the same circumstances as the original issuances. No samples of these instruments were found in the *Diario Oficial.* Scholars invariably refer to them as decrees with force of law.[41]

Under circumstances of foreign war or domestic strife, the president may, with the signature of all his cabinet ministers, declare that the public order has been disturbed and that, for that reason, the entire national territory or parts thereof are placed under a state of siege.[42] In this situation, the president may issue decrees to control the emergency. Although he may not repeal the national laws, he may suspend the effect of those that are incompatible with the state of siege. Consequently, once the government deems that public order has been reestablished all the special decrees issued under the state of siege cease, and the suspended statutes regain their legal force.[43]

Examination of the content of the *Diario Oficial* and the literature on the topic has revealed that these instruments may be identified under the heading *Decretos Legislativos* (legislative decrees). The charter also refers to them by the same designation.

Events other than those prescribed as legal grounds for the establishment of a state of siege, i.e., disturbances of or threats to the economic or social order, also constitute grounds for the president, with the signatures of all his cabinet ministers, to declare a state of emergency for periods which may not exceed ninety days in one year.[44] To avert the crisis, the president may issue decrees with force of law which must bear the signatures of all his cabinet ministers. These instruments are equivalent in legal strength to a law or ordinary statute and, in the opinion of one author, they could be repealed or amended by a subsequent law.[45]

Like the preceding special legislative issuances, it is not completely clear what designation these latter instruments may be found under in the *Diario Oficial* or in the official compilations. The constitution refers to this category as *decretos con fuerza de ley, decretos,* or *decretos legislativos.*[46] Samples of these decrees have not been located in the issues of the *Diario Oficial* examined.

Almost all decrees, be they ordinary or special, must bear the signatures of the president of the republic and the appropriate minister or ministers of the cabinet.[47] Furthermore, some of them must be signed by the president and all the ministers of the cabinet.[48] Finally, and in view of the fact that the constitution empowers the president to delegate some specific functions to ministers of the cabinet or other government officials, there may be cases where decrees have not borne the signature of the president.[49]

The official organ which publishes the text of decrees is the *Diario Oficial.*

Notes

1. Legislative Act No. 1 of December 18, 1975, *Diario Oficial* (*D.O.*) (January 21, 1976).
2. *Constitution of the Republic of Colombia, 1886* (Washington, D.C.: Organization of American States, 1971), art. 215 (hereafter cited as *Const.*).
3. Ibid., art. 218.
4. Ibid., art. 83, transitory paragraph.
5. J. Ortega Torres, *Código de régimen político y municipal (Ley 4a. de 1913 y normas legales complementarias),* 3rd ed. (Bogotá: TEMIS, 1973), art. 52 (hereafter cited as Ortega Torres, *Código*).
6. *Const.,* art. 120, no. 20.
7. Ibid., art. 76, no. 18.
8. A. Copete Lizarralde, *Lecciones de derecho constitucional colombiano, apuntes de clases* (Universidad Nacional de Colombia, 1951), p. 170.
9. A. Constaïn, *Elementos de derecho constitucional,* 3rd ed. (Bogotá: TEMIS, 1959), p. 173.
10. *Const.,* arts. 79-92.
11. Ibid., art. 56.
12. Ibid., art. 76.
13. Ibid , arts. 79 and 134.
14. Ibid., arts. 79, 182, and 208.
15. Ibid., art. 141, no. 2.
16. L. C. Sáchica, *Constitucionalismo colombiano,* 4th ed. (Bogotá: TEMIS, 1974), p. 475 (hereafter cited as Sáchica, *Const. col.*).
17. Ibid., arts. 72 and 79.
18. Ibid., art. 81.
19. Ibid., art. 85.
20. Ibid., art. 86.
21. Ibid., art. 87.
22. Ibid., art. 86.
23. Ibid., art. 88.
24. Ibid., art. 90.
25. Ibid., arts. 85, 86, and 89.
26. Ortega Torres, *Código,* arts. 52 and 53.
27. Sáchica, *Const. col.,* pp. 497 and 498.
28. Ibid., p. 495; *Const.,* arts. 76, 79, and 120.
29. *Const.,* arts. 76, no. 3 and 4; 187, no. 2; and 189.
30. Ibid., arts. 76, no. 4; and 80.
31. Ibid., arts. 120, no. 3; and 216; Sáchica, *Const. col.,* p. 439.
32. *Const.,* art. 120, nos. 12 and 14.
33. Sáchica, *Const. col.,* p. 439.
34. *Const.,* arts. 76, pars. 11 and 12; 80; 121; 122; et seq.

35. Sáchica, *Const. col.*, p. 460; G. Rojas Arbeláez, *El espíritu del derecho administrativo* (Bogotá: TEMIS, 1972), p. 85 (hereafter cited as Rojas Arbeláez, *Espíritu*).

36. Sáchica, *Const. col.*, p. 460; Rojas Arbeláez, *Espíritu*, p. 84.

37. *Const.*, art. 214, no. 2.

38. *Const.*, art. 76, no. 4.

39. Ibid., art. 80.

40. Ibid.

41. Sáchica, *Const. col.*, p. 437.

42. *Const.*, art. 121.

43. Ibid.

44. Ibid., art. 122.

45. Rojas Arbeláez, *Espíritu*, p. 85.

46. *Const.*, art. 122.

47. Ibid., art. 57.

48. Ibid., arts. 121 and 122.

49. Ibid., art. 135.

COSTA RICA

1. Constitution

2. Treaties

3. Law (Legislative) Accord

4. Decree [Executive] Accord Resolution

CONSTITUCIÓN (Constitution). The constitution currently in force in Costa Rica, enacted on November 7, 1949, by a popularly elected National Constituent Assembly, took effect on November 8, 1949. The last official text available was published in 1965.[1] The constitution has been amended several times.

The supremacy of the constitution over the entire legal system is clearly stated in the charter. Provisions enacted by the legislative or the executive powers which are contrary to the constitution are void.[2]

Control over the constitutionality of the statutory issuances of the legislative branch and decrees of the executive branch is entrusted to the Supreme Court of Justice. Other legal issuances of the executive are subject to the same control by judicial review.[3]

The supremacy of the constitution is further affirmed by the special procedure for its amendment. Amendments may be total or partial. The latter may be submitted by at least ten members of the Legislative Assembly. The amendatory bill shall then be published, assigned to a committee, and debated upon in the assembly. Approval of the bill requires a two-thirds vote of the membership. If approved, the committee drafts the bill again, and it is once more submitted to the decision of the assembly which now shall require only a majority vote for approval. The approved instrument is then forwarded to the president of the republic who shall consider and return it to the assembly in the following legislative term along with his objections or approval. The assembly shall submit the bill to three more debating sessions before a final vote. Approval requires the favorable vote of at least two-thirds of the membership again to integrate the new enactment into the constitutional text and have it "communicated to the executive branch for the corresponding publication and observance."[4]

The total amendment may only be undertaken by a constituent assembly convened for that special purpose by a law enacted by two-thirds of the Legislative Assembly. This law does not require the sanction of the executive power.[5] The relevant constitutional passage does not include any reference to the promulgation thereof as a responsibility of the executive in these cases.

Constitutional amendments must be published in the official newspaper, *La Gaceta.*

TRATADO INTERNACIONAL (International Treaty). According to the constitution, public treaties, international agreements, and concordats duly approved by the Legislative Assembly shall be higher in authority than the law from the moment they are published or from the date set forth therein.[6]

These instruments are negotiated by the president of the republic and the respective cabinet minister[7] and are forwarded to the Legislative Assembly for approval or rejection. If approved, the Legislative Assembly shall pass a law by observing the ordinary legislative procedure for enactments. International treaties and agreements which transfer certain competencies from the national level to an international legal system to carry out objectives of common regional concern shall require the approval of at least two-thirds of the entire membership.[8]

International instruments of a rank lower than, but derived from, international treaties and agreements already approved by the assembly shall not require legislative approval when they are generated under express instruction of the original treaty or agreement. In these cases, promulgation by means of a decree is the only requirement.[9]

In some special cases, the charter prescribes that certain treaties, agreements, or concordats shall require the approval of a constituent assembly rather than that of the Legislative Assembly. These special cases concern territorial integrity and the political organization of the country.[10]

Laws approving treaties, agreements, and concordats must be published in the official newspaper.[11]

An examination of randomly selected issues of *La Gaceta* revealed that, despite the constitutional provisions referred to, there are decrees which promulgate agreements apparently not derived from original international instruments, as prescribed. Perusal of related Costa Rican treatises and periodicals provided no additional information on the matter.

LEY (Law). According to the charter in force, the power to legislate resides in the people who delegate this power by means of suffrage to the Legislative Assembly.[12] Furthermore, the power to enact, amend, repeal, and give authentic interpretations to the law is vested exclusively in the Legislative Assembly[13] which may not delegate this responsibility.[14] Nevertheless, the executive branch plays an important role in the legislative enactment process, basically through the cabinet ministers.

A bill for a law may be introduced by any member of the Legislative Assembly or by the cabinet ministers of the executive branch,[15] the only exception being the bill containing the national budget which must be introduced solely by the president of the republic and his cabinet minister.[16]

Bills are subject to three separate debates.[17] Cabinet ministers may participate in the debating sessions but may not vote.[18] Bills may only be approved by the majority vote of those members attending the legislative session.[19] In some cases, however, the charter requires approval by two-thirds of the entire legislative membership for the passage of laws.[20] There are other cases in which the Legislative Assembly must consult with other bodies or entities during the lawmaking process. This requirement is prescribed for legislation concerning election, the university and institutions of higher education, and the organization and functions of the judiciary. Any departures shall only take place with the support of two-thirds of the assembly's membership.[21]

A bill approved by the Legislative Assembly becomes a *decreto legislativo* (legislative decree). Completion of the legislative process requires the sanctioning of the executive branch which may either approve or veto the decree within ten days. If no action is taken within this term, the executive shall sanction the decree into a law as if it were approved.[22]

If the executive vetoes a legislative decree, it must be reconsidered by the assembly and again approved by a two-thirds vote of its entire membership to override the presidential veto. If the veto is accepted, only a majority vote by the assembly will be required to endorse the executive objections.[23] Vetoes based on grounds of unconstitutionality must be submitted to the Supreme Court of Justice. If the court rules that the bill contains unconstitutional provisions it is defeated and may not be enacted.[24]

The charter grants the power to promulgate laws to the president of the republic who does so with the support of the respective cabinet minister.[25] Furthermore, the constitution provides that laws must be published in the official government newspaper.[26] Laws are enforceable ten days after their publication. Examination of a number of issues of this newspaper revealed that in fact laws are not assigned any specific heading in the printed version, only a serial number. Usually, a law may be identified as such by the number at the top of the text and a statement which reads, "The Legislative Assembly . . . decrees . . . ."

It is interesting to note that not only the laws were published in the official newspaper but that the bill submitted to the Legislative Assembly, the reports of the legislative commission to which the bill was assigned for preliminary consideration, and the presidential vetoes if any appeared as well.

The ordinary statute or law is subordinate to the constitution and to the international treaties and agreements entered into with foreign powers.[27]

ACUERDO (Accord). The Legislative Assembly has been granted other powers in addition to the typically legislative ones. These additional prerogatives are exercised by means of an instrument designated as an accord. The issuance of an accord presumably requires a majority vote in a single session; the constitutional passage does not refer to this aspect. Accords do not require sanctioning by the executive branch and are directly published in the official newspaper.[28] These instruments, according to the charter, are confined to such matters as designation of the premises where sessions shall be held, appointment of Supreme Court justices, granting or withholding consent for passages of foreign troops, authorization to the executive to declare a state of national defense, suspending (by the favorable vote of two-thirds of the entire membership) certain rights and guarantees established by the charter for the citizenry, and a number of other areas specifically enumerated therein.[29] Despite this enumeration in the constitution, accords covering other matters have been published in the official newspaper.

As in the case of the laws, these published instruments cannot be identified by a direct heading at the top of the text. They are regularly preceded by the statement, "The Legislative Assembly . . . accords . . . ."

It is important to note that this designation has not been assigned to the issuances of the Legislative Assembly exclusively. Accords may also be found as issuances of the Board of the Legislative Assembly and the executive branch.

Accords and laws coexist separately at the same authority level. Theoretically, there should be no interference between the two because they are supposed to control different matters. Both laws and accords are directly subordinate to the constitution and the international treaties.

DECRETO (Decree). The executive power is vested in the president of the republic and his cabinet ministers.[30] Nevertheless, these officials may perform their duties in a variety of ways: the president by himself, the president and one cabinet minister, or the president and all his cabinet ministers as a unit designated *Consejo de Gobierno* (Council of Government).[31]

Examination of the constitutional provisions suggests that the most significant powers granted to the executive branch can only be exercised with the support of one or more cabinet ministers. These powers include the promulgation, implementation, and regulation of laws; suspension of established rights and guarantees under special and restricted circumstances; and promulgation of international treaties and agreements as laws of the land.[32]

Samples of the official newspaper revealed that whenever the president acts in conjunction with one or more of his cabinet ministers the statement at the head of the instrument issued reads, "The President of the Republic and the Minister . . . Decree . . . ." On the other hand, the official source refers to these instruments as executive decrees. They always display a serial number accompanied by a capital letter; the latter is the initial corresponding to the cabinet ministry to which they are related.

There can be no certainty as to the correct legal designation of these instruments. Neither the law, the literature, nor the practice indicate that a specific title heading or headings are assigned.

Regarding authority rank of the executive decrees, all executive branch functions must conform to the laws, the international treaties and agreements, and finally to the constitution. There is an administrative court with special jurisdiction to ensure such conformity.[33]

ACUERDO [EJECUTIVO] ([Executive] Accord). When the president exercises his executive prerogatives by himself, he operates through an accord. The printed version of this instrument displays no heading; instead there is an opening statement which reads, "The President of the Republic accords . . . ." Some of the functions to be performed by the president alone include appointing and dismissing cabinet ministers and exercising the supreme command of the police force.[34] This category of executive instrument also lacks informative material which prevents full interpretation.

The executive accords are subordinate to the laws, the international treaties and agreements, and finally to the constitution.[35] There is no information available at this time concerning conflicts between accords and decrees or any other instrument issued at the executive level.

RESOLUCIÓN (Resolution). Under certain circumstances, the president is required to act with the support of his entire cabinet. As previously stated, this unit has been designated the Council of Government. Apparently, the council does not issue any legislative instrument by itself, rather it is the president of the republic and the minister of the presidency who issue the instrument implementing the Council of Government's decision. Only one sample of this instrument was found in the official gazettes reviewed. This accord concerned the exercise of the right to pardon. The opening statement of the instrument read, "The President of the Republic and the Minister of the Presidency, pursuant to the decision of the Council of Government, Resolve . . . ." It seems probable then that this instrument be designated a resolution.

This instrument shares the authority rank of the decree and executive accord. There is no information as to which of the three shall prevail in case of conflict.[36]

Notes

1. *Constitution of the Republic of Costa Rica, 1949 (As Amended)* (Washington, D.C.: Organization of American States, 1965) (hereafter cited as *Const.*).
2. Ibid., art. 10.
3. Ibid., art. 10, pars. 2 and 3.
4. Ibid., art. 195.
5. Ibid., art. 196.
6. Ibid., art. 7.
7. Ibid., art. 140, no. 10.
8. Ibid., arts. 121, no. 4; and 124.
9. Ibid., art. 121, no. 4, par. 3.
10. Ibid., arts. 140, no. 10; and 7, par. 2.
11. Ibid., art. 124.
12. Ibid., art. 105.
13. Ibid., art. 121, no. 1.
14. Ibid., art. 9.
15. Ibid., arts. 123; and 140, no. 5.
16. Ibid., arts. 140, no. 15; and 178.
17. Ibid., art. 124.
18. Ibid., art. 145.
19. *Reglamento de orden, dirección y disciplina interior de la Asamblea Legislativa* (San José: Imprenta Nacional, 1955), art. 48.
20. *Const.*, arts. 46; 96e; 97; 121, no. 15; and 167.
21. Ibid., arts. 88, 97, and 167.
22. Ibid., arts. 124; 126; and 140, no. 5.
23. Ibid., art. 127.
24. Ibid., art. 128.
25. Ibid., art. 140, no. 3.
26. Ibid., arts. 124, 126, and 129.
27. Ibid., arts. 7 and 10.
28. Ibid., art. 124.
29. Ibid.
30. Ibid., art. 130.
31. Ibid., arts. 139, 140, and 147.
32. Ibid., art. 140.
33. Ibid., arts. 10 and 49.
34. Ibid., art. 139.
35. Ibid., arts. 10 and 49.
36. Ibid.

CUBA

1. Constitution

2. Law Treaties Decree Law

3. Decree Ministerial Resolution

The research for this section has been affected by two basic problems. The first is the alarmingly scarce amount of information available of either a primary or secondary nature, be it from official, academic, or private sources. The second is that rather recently Cuba has enacted a new constitution establishing a governmental structure different from that set up by the previous charter. There is little or no literature available as yet on the newest constitution. These basic difficulties have seriously confined the scope, depth, and accuracy of this section; therefore, the instruments enumerated, their description, and related commentaries are limited and tentative.

CONSTITUCIÓN (Constitution). Cuba's current constitution was enacted by proclamation of the Council of Ministers after approval by referendum on February 15, 1976.[1] A transitory law was also approved and enacted to control the transition from the former constitution to the present one[2] and to provide for the gradual enforcement of the new charter. The preamble of the constitution and articles 1 to 65, 69, 100, and 134 to 141 were to take effect on February 24, 1976. Articles 101 to 120 were to come into force after election of delegates to the Municipal Assemblies. The rest of the new charter was to be enforced as soon as the supreme organs of the popular power were constituted.[3] Currently all the provisions of the Constitution of 1976 are in force.

The constitution prevails over all other legislative instruments. Constitutional conformity is controlled by the National Assembly, the Council of State, or the Council of Ministers.[4]

Amendments to the constitution may be either partial or total and must be made according to the special procedures prescribed by the charter. A partial amendment may be conducted by the National Assembly and requires at least a two-thirds vote. A total amendment, or amendments related to the integration and powers of the National Assembly of the Popular Power or its Council of State or to the rights and duties established by the constitution also require approval by the majority of the nation's citizens by referendum as conducted by the National Assembly.[5] All amendments must be published in the official newspaper, *Gaceta Oficial.*

LEY (Law). According to the constitution, the National Assembly of the People's Power is the only state national entity vested with legislative authority.[6] Bills may be introduced by the deputies to the National Assembly of the People's Power, the Council of State, the Council of Ministers, the commissions of the National Assembly of the People's Power, the National Committee of the Central Organization of Cuban Trade Unions and the national offices of the other social and mass organizations, the People's Supreme Court through its Council of Government on matters concerning the administration of justice, the office of the attorney general on matters within its competence, or the citizenry, at least ten thousand qualified voters.[7]

Laws are enacted by a simple majority of votes. Nevertheless, the National Assembly may decide to submit bills to a national referendum before enactment depending on the nature of the issue or issues involved.[8] No further procedure is prescribed by the charter, and there are no other regulations available at this time.

Laws approved by the National Assembly go into effect on the date determined by the laws themselves in each case. These instruments must be signed by the president of the National Assembly and published in the official newspaper by his order.[9]

Several provisions in the charter reserve the regulation of certain matters for the law. Some of these are the establishment of agencies to deal with international trade, the implementation of the socialist labor principle—"from each person according to his own capability, to each person according to his work"—private ownership of land by small farmers and other related personal property matters, and inheritance rights vis-à-vis owned dwellings.[10]

Concerning the authority rank of the laws, they must conform and are subordinate to the constitution. Issues concerning the constitutionality of laws are decided by the National Assembly.[11]

DECRETO LEY (Decree Law). The National Assembly of the People's Power holds two ordinary sessions a year and as many special sessions as requested by at least one-third of its membership or by the Council of the State.[12] During its recess, the National Assembly is represented by the Council of State, a thirty-one-member body elected by the assembly from among its own deputies.[13] The Council of State exercises a number of specific powers, the issuing of decree laws being one of them.[14]

According to the pertinent constitutional passages, the Council of State adopts its legislative instruments by a simple majority of favorable votes.[15] No provisions have been found regarding the specific procedure for issuing decree laws.

Decree laws are signed by the president of the Council of State, and publication in the official newspaper is required.[16]

This instrument must be in conformity with the constitution. Control of such conformity is entrusted by the charter to the National Assembly which may repeal decree laws by ruling them inapplicable.[17]

TRATADO INTERNACIONAL (International Treaty). This instrument is negotiated by the Council of Ministers. Once concluded, it is submitted to the Council of State for ratification. The council is also empowered to denounce a treaty.[18] There were no other provisions or information available concerning the authority rank of instruments in this category. No references have been found concerning past practices and policies either.

DECRETO (Decree). The constitution states that the Council of Ministers is the highest ranking executive and administrative organ and constitutes the government of the republic.[19] This council may issue decrees for the implementation of existing laws and supervise their enforcement. Likewise, the Council of Ministers is empowered to issue regulations to implement not only the existing laws but also the resolutions of the National Assembly, the decree laws, and related instruments issued by the Council of State.[20]

Decrees are subordinate to decree laws, laws, and ultimately to the constitution. Control of conformance to this ranking scale is the responsibility of the National Assembly which may repeal any violating instrument.[21]

Notes

1. *Constitución de la República de Cuba*, official ed. (La Habana: Editorial Orbe, Instituto Cubano del Libro, February 1976) (hereafter cited as *Const.*).
2. Ibid.
3. Transitory Law (supra), art. 1.
4. *Const.*, arts. 73c, r, and s; 88ñ and o; and 96n.
5. Ibid., art. 141.
6. Ibid., arts. 68 and 73b.
7. Ibid., arts. 86, 96g, 98c, and 124.
8. Ibid., art. 74.
9. Ibid., arts. 75 and 79ch.
10. Ibid., arts. 18, 19, 20, 24, and 25.
11. Ibid., art. 73c.
12. Ibid., art. 76.
13. Ibid., arts. 72 and 87.
14. Ibid., art. 88c.
15. Ibid., art. 89.
16. Ibid., arts. 91h, and 75.
17. Ibid., art. 73c and r.
18. Ibid., arts. 88n and 96ch.
19. Ibid., art. 93.
20. Ibid., art. 96k and j.
21. Ibid., art. 73c and r.

DOMINICAN REPUBLIC

1. Constitution
2. Law Treaties Resolution
3. Decree

Dominican Republic

CONSTITUCIÓN (Constitution). After a period of national political unrest in 1965, the Dominican National Congress issued a law converting itself into a National Assembly for the purpose of solving what was thought to be the country's constitutional problem.[1] A decree issued by the president of the republic set into motion the National Assembly[2] which repealed the Constitution of 1963 and enacted by proclamation the new Constitution of November 28, 1966.[3]

The supremacy of the constitution over all other legislative instruments was expressly prescribed in the charter: "Any law, decree, resolution, regulation or act contrary to this constitution shall be null and void *ipso jure.*"[4] One scholar stated that this nullity must be judicially declared despite the fact that the charter docs not specifically assign this power to any given branch of the government.[5] Aside from this there is no literature available on the charter of 1966.

Consonant with western constitutional traditions, the legal supremacy of the constitution requires that special procedures be observed for its amendment. First of all, a law is required to declare the need to amend the charter. The corresponding bill may be submitted by either the executive branch or by one-third of the members of either of the two legislative bodies.[6] The enacted law shall provide for holding a meeting of the National Assembly and defining the purpose of the amendment including the constitutional articles which will be affected.[7]

The National Assembly shall meet within fifteen days following the publication of the law to state the need for the constitutional amendment. Quorum for this meeting of the assembly consists of attendance of more than half of the members of each legislative body composing the assembly. Once the National Assembly has voted and proclaimed the amendment, the constitution shall be published in its entirety including the amended texts. For an amendment to succeed, a favorable vote by two-thirds of the attending members is required.[8] Amendments concerning the form of government are forbidden by the charter.[9]

The publication referred to above is performed by the official newspaper, *Gaceta Oficial,* as prescribed by the Civil Code. Publication in other widely circulating newspapers is also authorized by the law when so expressed in the corresponding instrument. The executive branch is empowered to issue orders for unofficial publication sources.[10] Despite these rather clear provisions, legislative instruments have been published in extraofficial sources even when the executive has expressly ordered that they be published only in the official newspaper. It is recommended that readers conducting studies in this jurisdiction be prepared to search for additional sources when looking for statutory material. For example, Law no. 17 of September 13, 1966, transforming the National Congress into the National Assembly in order to decide on a new constitution was published in the newspapers, *El Caribe* and *Listín Diario.*

The final text of the amended constitution is not promulgated by the president, but by the National Assembly itself. The published version does not bear the heading Law or a serial number. It may be located under the direct heading Constitution.

LEY (Law). The charter provides that the exercise of the legislative power is entrusted to the Congress of the republic which consists of two bodies, the Senate and the Chamber of Deputies.[11] Congress has, therefore, the power to legislate on all matters that are not expressly entrusted to another agency.[12] The rank of this legislative instrument is also determined by the charter itself which further provides that no laws may be issued contrary to the constitution.[13]

A bill for a law may be submitted by members of either legislative body, the president of the republic, the Supreme Court of Justice on matters concerning the judiciary, and by the Central Electoral Board on matters concerning elections.[14] The president of the republic has the exclusive privilege of submitting the bill on the national budget.[15]

Debates on bills may be initiated in either legislative body and must be debated upon twice in separate sessions in both the Senate and the Chamber of Deputies. Disagreements between these two bodies may result in additional debating sessions. If after these debates the bill fails to be approved by Congress it is rejected. Bills may be submitted as urgent and so declared by Congress, in which case the number of debates allowed is shortened.[16] Legislative decision to enact a law is made by a favorable vote of the majority of the attending members. Bills submitted and declared urgent need a two-thirds favorable vote in the second discussion. Such matters as banking and public expenditures also require special portions of favorable voting for their enactment.[17] After a bill has been approved by Congress, it is forwarded to the executive. At this juncture, the president may either object to it or approve it within eight days. If objected to, the bill is returned to Congress for further debate. A two-thirds favorable vote is required in each body for Congress to override the presidential veto.[18]

Laws are promulgated by the president of the republic who shall add a promulgatory statement at the end of the basic congressional text.[19] Customarily, the date of the law is taken to be that of its promulgation rather than that of congressional enactment.[20]

This legislative instrument may be identified by its opening statement, "The National Congress, in the name of the republic . . . ."[21] Laws are published in the official newspaper, *Gaceta Oficial,* or in other newspapers of wide circulation when the law so states or the executive so orders.[22]

Laws are binding on the first day after their publication in the national district, and the second day after publication in the rest of the territory.[23] It is considered that by then the law is known to everyone within the national territory.

Despite the above requirements, samples of laws have been found that have been issued by de facto governments with no congressional participation.

RESOLUCIÓN (Resolution). Besides typical legislative powers the National Congress has apparently exercised other powers by means of an instrument known as a resolution. A Dominican legal scholar states that resolutions require only one discussion in each legislative body. He cites no authority in support of his proposition,[24] and no constitutional provision has been found to this effect. Furthermore, neither the charter nor legal literary sources indicate the kind of congressional actions assigned to the content of the resolution. Nevertheless, resolutions, when issued, are also published following the same procedures prescribed for laws.[25]

There is no indication of the resolution's ranking authority except a general statement concerning the requirement of a resolution's conformity with the constitution under penalty of nullity.[26]

Finally, resolutions have been found issued by de facto government in the absence of a congress or by a person acting as a provisional president.

TRATADO INTERNACIONAL (International Treaty). The constitution provides that the president of the republic has the power to conclude treaties with foreign powers and international organizations.[27] These instruments, however, require congressional approval,[28] ordinarily through a resolution, and are then published according to the formal requirement detailed in the preceding section.

The charter does not refer to the authority rank of international treaties within the Dominican legal system. Nevertheless, the same scholar cited above states that they rank equally with laws or ordinary statutes. Consequently, if an international treaty contradicts an existing law, the latter shall be rendered inapplicable and vice versa. The author claims that his position is based on Dominican practices and on comparative studies of similar legal systems.[29]

DECRETO (Decree). Under the charter, the executive power is entrusted to the president of the republic[30] who performs his basic functions through decrees. The pertinent constitutional passage states that the president may issue regulations, decrees, and instructions whenever they are deemed necessary.[31] Examination of a number of issues of the official newspaper reveals that even when the president issues regulatory instruments they are in the format, under the designation, and with a serial number of a decree. It is of no surprise then to find that decrees, in fact, vary in content. In some cases, decrees cover matters usually reserved for the law but under limited circumstances, in which case they must be submitted for congressional approval.[32] These instruments are issued solely with the signature of the president of the republic. Cabinet ministers are not required to countersign the document.

Publication of the decrees is required under the general provisions of the Civil Code.[33]

Regarding the authority rank of the decrees, the charter provides that all presidential acts are required to conform to the laws and ultimately the constitution. The National Congress is entrusted by the charter itself with the task of controlling this conformity and subordination.[34]

Notes

1. Law no. 17 of September 13, 1966, *El Caribe* (*E.C.*) and *Listín Diario* (*L.D.*) (September 14, 1966), and *Gaceta Oficial* (*G.O.*) (September 21, 1966).
2. Decree 319 of September 15, 1966, *G.O.* (September 21, 1966).
3. *Constitución de la República Dominicana, votada y proclamada por la Asamblea Nacional en fecha 28 de noviembre de 1966, G.O.* (November 29, 1966) (Santo Domingo: Imprenta J. R. Vda. García Sucesores, 1966) (hereafter cited as *Const.*).
4. Ibid., art. 46.
5. M. A. Amiama, *Notas sobre derecho constitucional* (Ciudad Trujillo: Montalvo, 1954), p. 103 (hereafter cited as Amiama, *Notas*).
6. *Const.*, art. 116.
7. Ibid., art. 117.
8. Ibid., art. 118.
9. Ibid., art. 119.
10. *Código Civil*, 2d ed. (Madrid: Gráficas Meri, 1971) art. 1. (hereafter cited as *C. Civ.*).
11. *Const.*, art. 16.
12. Ibid., art. 37, no. 23.
13. Ibid., art. 46.
14. Ibid., art. 38.
15. Ibid., art. 55, no. 23.
16. Ibid., arts. 38, 39, and 40.
17. Ibid., arts. 112 and 115, pars. 2 and 3.
18. Ibid., art. 41.
19. Ibid., arts. 41 and 55, no. 2.
20. Amiama, *Notas*, p. 102.
21. *Const.*, art. 44.
22. Ibid., art. 45; *C. Civ.*, art. 1.
23. Ibid.
24. Amiama, *Notas*, p. 97.
25. *C. Civ.*, art. 1.
26. *Const.*, art. 46.
27. Ibid., art. 55, no. 6.
28. Ibid., art. 37, no. 14.
29. Amiama, *Notas*, p. 121.
30. *Const.*, art. 49.
31. Ibid., art. 55, no. 2.
32. Ibid., art. 115, par. V.
33. *C. Civ.*, art.1.
34. *Const.*, arts. 37, no. 18; and 46.

ECUADOR

Under the Constitution

1. Constitution

2. Law   Decree Law   Treaties   (Legislative) Decree

3. (Executive) Decree

Current Status

1. Constitution   Decree

2. Treaties   Accord

CONSTITUCIÓN (Constitution). The Ecuadorian constitution currently in force was reenacted by a decree issued by the general commanders of the army, navy, and air force on January 11, 1976.[1] This charter has been previously sanctioned by the National Constituent Assembly, and promulgated by decree on March 6, 1945,[2] but was short-lived. The Decree of January 11, 1976, stated that the constitution will be enforced only when not interfering with the objectives set forth by the government.

The supremacy of the constitution over all other forms of legislative instruments is conspicuously stressed throughout its text.[3] One of the provisions states that the constitution is the supreme law of the republic; therefore, laws, decrees, ordinances, regulations, agreements, orders, provisions, pacts, or public treaties that are either in opposition to or amendatory of it shall be void.[4] The task of controlling the constitutionality of official actions is entrusted to the Congress.[5]

Another constitutional precept provides that the charter shall not be amended within four years after its promulgation.[6] When an amendment is admissible, it must be considered by two different congressional terms, that is, different congresses. The first Congress considering the amendment shall debate on the bill as if it were an ordinary legislative draft. Once approved, it is forwarded to the president of the republic who shall publish it with his report. The second Congress considering the bill either approves or rejects the amendatory proposal by a two-thirds vote. If approved by Congress, the president of the republic cannot object to the amendment and is obligated to promulgate it.[7]

Current Status. The general commanders of the army, navy, and air force established themselves by decree in a Supreme Council of Government and took control of the country.[8] The Constitution of 1945, brought back into force by the general commanders, was given authority as far as it was compatible with the new objectives set forth by the military. These circumstances and the abolition of Congress significantly reduced the scope of the charter. The abolition of Congress and the electoral process rendered most of the fundamental constitutional structure of government inoperative. The new government also determined that the procedure for constitutional amendment was no longer in force. The content of decree no. 1 may very well have led to the repeal of passages of the charter by legislative instruments issued by the Supreme Council of Government. Since there is no heading indicating the constitutional nature of these instruments, the reader will need to consider the content of each of them when looking for basic sources of law under the current Ecuadorian legal system.

No provisions have been found covering the exercise of constituent power under these circumstances. Examination of the official newspaper did not reveal legislative instruments other than laws and decrees, both issuances of the Supreme Council of Government.

LEY; DECRETO (Law; Decree). According to the Ecuadorian constitution, the legislative power is entrusted to the National Congress which consists of a single body.[9] A national legal scholar has stated there is more than one legislative instrument issued by congress.[10] The constitution makes reference to four different kinds of issuances: law, decree, accord, and resolution.[11]

There are no definitions in the charter concerning laws or decrees. It is difficult to furnish a concept for each because the current charter had a rather ephemeral existence at the time of its original enactment in 1945, and under the present circumstances the passages affecting the legislature are not in force. Comparisons between the printed versions of these instruments revealed no apparent substantive or formal differences. Decrees modify laws or codes, and vice versa;[12] format and procedures are also identical. In both cases under the constitution the initiative to introduce bills may be exercised by any member of the legislature, the president of the republic, the Permanent Legislative Commission, and the Supreme Court on matters concerning civil, criminal, procedural, and judicial matters.[13]

After a bill is approved by a legislative committee it is subjected to two debates, except when drafted by the Permanent Legislative Commission when only one debate is required.[14] One or more members of the Supreme Court may participate in the debates of the bills it introduces.[15]

Once approved by Congress, a bill is forwarded to the president of the republic for approval or veto. Whatever the action taken by him, the bill must return to Congress within eight days ordinarily, or within three days when the bill bears a note of urgency. Should the president of the republic not take any action within the prescribed term, the bill becomes enforceable.[16]

If the legislative term expires before the time granted to the president, the latter shall publish the bill with his objections, if any, in the official newspaper and shall present it to the next Congress within the first three days of session. Should the president fail to do so, the bill gains force of law.[17]

In cases of presidential veto, Congress ordinarily debates on the objections in one session. Objections may be accepted in whole or in part, or Congress may insist on its original version.[18] There are no constitutional provisions concerning what vote is required to override presidential vetoes. An Ecuadorian scholar suggests that in that case the general rule of a majority decision of the legislative body will apply, that is, a favorable vote of the majority of the entire membership is required.[19]

If presidential objections are based on grounds of unconstitutionality, and Congress disagrees with his arguments, the bill concerned shall be forwarded to the Tribunal of Constitutional Guarantees for a decision.[20]

Laws and decrees are to be promulgated by the president of the republic within ten days of their congressional approval. Failing this, the Permanent Legislative Commission promulgates.[21] Promulgation is carried out by inserting the instrument in the *Registro Oficial,* with the date of promulgation being that of publication. Laws, decrees, and accords related to national defense and considered confidential are inserted in a special separate issue of the official newspaper.[22]

According to the law, legislative instruments become enforceable six days after the date of publication in the capital city and one day later for each twenty kilometers of distance from that city for the rest of the territory.[23] Laws and decrees are directly subordinate to the constitution.[24]

An interesting category of laws, called codified laws, exists in Ecuador. These instruments are basically an integrated systematic version of a number of legislative instruments enacted at different times on a given subject by the Permanent Legislative Commission composed of ten members, some appointed by Congress and others by the president. Essentially restatements of laws integrated in one body, they are ranked with ordinary laws or statutes.[25]

Current Status. When the Supreme Council of Government seized control of the government in January 1976, the Congress had already been dismissed, allowing the Supreme Council to seize legislative power. The *Comisión Legislativa,* or Legislative Committee, a body established in 1972 to assist the previous de facto government in its basic legislative task, was maintained. This commission, which resembles the Permanent Legislative Commission of the 1945 Constitution, was created by Decree 1395-A, published in the *Registro Oficial* of December 1, 1972. By provision, its members were to be appointed by the president of the republic, but actually the Supreme Council exercises this task.

The Supreme Council issues laws and decrees which display the same format and appear to treat the same subjects covered by instruments with similar designations under the Constitution of 1945. These issuances are also published in the official gazette. The Legislative Committee is entrusted with the preparation of the codified laws and approves the bills drafted by the ministers of the cabinet which are forwarded to the Supreme Council for enactment.

Legislative instruments currently issued by the Supreme Council of Government are designated decrees. Examination of the *Registro Oficial* supports this assertion. The designation law or code may sometimes be displayed as a subheading.

No provisions were found concerning authority rank of these instruments. Since the constitution is only in force when it does not oppose the government's objectives it appears that decrees issued by the Supreme Council of Government are not subordinate to the constitution and therefore, are not subject to conformance.

TRATADO INTERNACIONAL (International Treaty). The charter provides that the president of the republic has the power to negotiate treaties and other international agreements that are not in opposition to the constitution. After congressional approval, the president ratifies them and exchanges the pertinent instrument with the corresponding foreign powers.[26] Congressional approval is indicated by legislative decrees.[27]

It is clear that international instruments must conform to the constitution.[28] No other reference has been found regarding the hierarchical relationship between these instruments and other legislative or executive issuances.

Current Status. Considerable examination of the *Registro Oficial* did not reveal a systematic use of specific instruments for ratification, promulgation, enactment, and approval, which are separate and distinct processes affecting international treaties. Sometimes a decree issued by the Supreme Council of Government did bring into effect a given international treaty or agreement. At another time, a decree issued by the same body was promulgated to meet the ratification requirement. Finally, international treaties were found published without a legislative instrument issued to approve or ratify them. This category may indeed be confusing to the researcher seeking consistency and order in the legal systems.

DECRETO-LEY (Decree Law). The Permanent Legislative Commission is empowered by the charter to issue decree laws on matters of an urgent nature concerning the economy of the nation during the congressional recess. The charter further requires that such decree laws be issued in agreement with the president of the republic and with the support of the National Economic Commission. Although these decree laws carry the force of ordinary statutes or laws, they may be repealed by a simple congressional resolution.[29] Their level of hierarchy is therefore subordinate to the latter and ultimately to the constitution. In the copies of the *Registro Oficial* scanned, samples of this instrument were not available for examination and further identification.

DECRETO (Decree). The charter entrusts the president of the republic with the responsibility of issuing regulations to legislative issuances, laws, and decrees, provided that these regulations do not oppose or alter the original legislative sources.[30]

Regulations and other instruments issued by the president in pursuance of his competence are, by the large, designated decrees. They are required to bear the signature of the president and the countersignature of the corresponding cabinet minister for enforceability.[31] They may carry provisions that are either general or specific and private in nature. In hierarchy, they are subordinate to the ordinary legislative statutes or laws and decrees.[32]

Current Status. At present the Supreme Council of Government has assumed all the executive and legislative functions. Since all issuances of this governmental body are released as decrees, it is materially impossible to discern which decrees correspond to the different areas of the former constitutional scheme.

Another instrument, the accord, was found by examining the *Registro Oficial*. This instrument originates at the cabinet level and its content suggests it replaces the executive decree which was prescribed by the Constitution of 1945.

Notes

1. Decree no. 1 of January 11, 1976, *Registro Oficial* (*R.O.*) (January 12, 1976) (hereafter cited as Decree no. 1).

2. *Constitución Política de la República del Ecuador* (Quito: Talleres Gráficos Nacionales, 1945) (hereafter cited as *Const.*).

3. Ibid., arts. 163; 164; 165; 35, no. 1; 66, no. 1; 160, nos. 2, 3, and 4.

4. Ibid., art. 163.

5. Ibid., art. 165.

6. Ibid., art. 166.

7. Ibid., arts. 34, no. 2; and 166.

8. Decree no. 1.

9. *Const.*, art. 23.

10. R. Borja y Borja, *Derecho constitucional ecuatoriano* (Madrid: Ediciones Cultura Hispánica, 1950), 1:330 (hereafter cited as Borja y Borja, *Derecho*).

11. *Const.*, art. 34, no. 3.

12. See, for example, *R.O.* (February 18, 1976, and June 14, 1976).

13. *Const.*, art. 36.

14. Ibid., arts. 37 and 54.

15. Ibid., art. 90.

16. Ibid., arts. 37, 38, and 40.

17. Ibid., art. 42.

18. Ibid., art. 39.

19. Borja y Borja, *Derecho*, p. 348.

20. *Const.*, art. 41.

21. Ibid., art. 46.

22. *Código Civil*, *R.O.* (November 20, 1970, suplemento del no. 104, 7th ed.).

23. Ibid., art. 6.

24. *Const.*, art. 163.

25. Ibid., arts. 49 and 63.

26. Ibid., art. 65, no. 4.

27. Ibid., art. 34, no. 5.

28. Ibid., arts. 163 and 165.

29. Ibid., art. 53, no. 2.

30. Ibid., art. 65, no. 2.

31. Ibid., art. 75.

32. Ibid., art. 160, no. 2.

Guatemala

1. Constitution
2. (Legislative) Decree Treaties
3. (Executive) Decree Accord

CONSTITUCIÓN (Constitution). The supremacy of the constitution is established by the charter currently in force. It was enacted by a Constituent National Assembly on September 15, 1965, to take effect on May 5, 1966. Many passages relate to the question of constitutional supremacy.[1] The more directly relevant passages provide that no law may be contrary to the constitution, and that the courts of justice of the nation shall always observe the principle that the constitution prevails over laws and international treaties. Laws in violation of the preceding principle are null and void *ipso jure.*[2] Control of constitutional conformity of laws and all other legislative instruments, including such executive initiatives as accords and decrees, is entrusted to the Court of Constitutionality whose decisions render unconstitutional legislative instruments ineffective. The court's decisions may affect the instrument concerned partially or totally and take effect on the day following the date of the decision's publication in the official daily.[3]

Special procedures are set forth for amending the charter depending on basic areas of concern. If the amendment proposed deals with Guatemala's full or partial participation in a Union of Central America or incorporation of Belize into the Guatemalan territory it may be undertaken by the unicameral Congress and the Council of State jointly with the approval of two-thirds of both bodies.[4] Another area relates to the noneligibility for reelection of the president of the republic, which is not subject to amendment under the Guatemalan charter.[5] Other amendments may be introduced by Congress convening, by a two-thirds vote, the National Constituent Assembly, which must approve the amendment. The instrument convening the National Assembly is a legislative decree which indicates the specific passages or provisions to be affected by the amendment.[6] Constitutional amendments are published in the official newspaper.

DECRETO (Decree). The power to legislate is vested in the Congress of the republic, according to the Guatemalan charter. Congress is a single body entrusted with a number of functions including the power to enact, amend, and repeal legislation.[7] Examination of the official daily reveals that Congress discharges its major functions through the decree even though the constitution does not refer to the decree. Also missing are provisions concerning the manner of issuing decrees. Instead, the charter explains in considerable detail the stages of enactment of the *ley*, or law, which is only one type of legal instrument that the decree may carry for promulgation. The charter does not indicate if these stages are also observed to enact decrees with other content than is assigned to laws. After observation and consideration of a number of decrees it appears that the standards for a law apply to all other forms of legislative instruments issued by Congress. Laws may be introduced by members of Congress, the ministers of the executive cabinet on matters concerning their areas of responsibility, the Council of State, the Supreme Court of Justice on matters concerning its own competence, and the University of San Carlos of Guatemala.[8] Bills on the national budget are the prerogative of the executive branch.[9]

Ordinarily, bills must undergo congressional debate at three different sessions. Under extraordinary emergency circumstances and by decision of two-thirds of Congress, the number of sessions may be reduced.[10] Ordinary decisions are made by a majority vote.[11] The charter describes a number of circumstances and categories for which a different proportion of favorable voting is required. For example, laws classified as constitutional, presumably because of their substance, require a two-thirds vote of the congressional membership to be amended.[12] Participation of the Council of State is sometimes mandatory in this process,[13] but at other times its participation comes at the request of the president of Congress or of five deputies of Congress. Members of the Council of State and the Congress may form a joint committee to decide on a bill which has been rejected or not acted upon congressionally within the prescribed term.[14]

Bills approved by Congress are ordinarily forwarded to the executive for sanction and promulgation. The president of the republic with cabinet support of the Council of Ministers may object to the bill within fifteen days. The bill thus vetoed returns to Congress for reconsideration. The opinion of the Council of State is required on the matter before Congress decides whether to ratify its original stand or accept the executive veto. Congressional ratification requires a two-thirds vote to override the veto.[15] In either case, the president of the republic must sanction and promulgate the law within eight days. Should he fail to do so, Congress will order that the corresponding publication become a law of the republic.[16]

Executive approval is not required for congressional legislative instruments passed for internal legislative activities and on matters entrusted exclusively to Congress by the charter.[17]

Laws take effect eight days after their publication in the Guatemalan official daily, but this term may be altered by the provisions of the law itself.[18]

Laws are subordinate to the constitution.[19] No direct references were found regarding the rank of decrees within the system. The general context of the Guatemalan charter and the traditional broad interpretation of the term law may very well comprise all instruments, like the decrees, which carry general and enforceable provisions under the same category.

TRATADO INTERNACIONAL (International Treaty). The Guatemalan charter prescribes that international treaties, conventions, and agreements are submitted by the president of the republic for approval by the National Congress by a decree.[20] Congressional approval of international instruments may require a different vote depending on the subject in question. When the international instrument affects laws currently in force which needed a two-thirds vote for passage, it will require the same proportion of votes for approval. A two-thirds vote is also required to approve treaties concerning subjects specified in the charter.[21]

Ordinarily, a majority vote of the legislature is sufficient for enactment of laws approving other types of international treaties.[22] Treaties and other international instruments are ratified by the president of the republic by means of an instrument which has not been assigned a designation or serial number. The minister of foreign affairs is required to countersign these instruments, which are published in the official daily like other statutory instruments.

International instruments are subordinate to the constitution.[23] The ranking relationships between treaties and ordinary laws is not completely clear. A constitutional provision, however, suggests that they are at least equated with ordinary laws.[24]

ACUERDO; DECRETO EJECUTIVO (Accord; Executive Decree). The charter provides that executive power is exercised by the president of the republic whose every action requires support from either his entire cabinet or its individual members, depending on the circumstances.[25] This exercise is performed by means of decrees, accords, regulations, and orders.[26] All of them must be issued in accordance and compliance with the ordinary laws.[27]

Examination of legislative indexes shows that the president of the republic actually issues decrees and accords. No reference has been found, however, concerning the differences between these two categories. Format, subject matter, and procedures seem to be quite similar, if not identical. The only variation is that decrees carry a serial number, but accords do not.

Because of their authority rank, decrees and accords may not oppose the law and shall always be issued in pursuance thereof.[28] Therefore, they appear directly subordinate to ordinary laws and ultimately to the constitution.

Notes

1. R. Azurdia Alfaro, *Constitución de la República de Guatemala decretada por la Asamblea Nacional Constituyente en 15 de Septiembre de 1965*, 9th ed. (Guatemala: Ministerio de Gobernación, 1965) (hereafter cited as Azurdia Alfaro, *Const.*); also published in *El Guatemalteco* (*E.G.*) (September 15, 1965).
2. Azurdia Alfaro, *Const.*, arts. 172 and 246.
3. Ibid., arts. 263 and 265; in 1972 the official gazette, *El Guatemalteco*, was renamed *Diario de Centro America*.
4. Azurdia Alfaro, *Const.*, art. 266.
5. Ibid., art. 267.
6. Ibid., arts. 266, 268, and 269.
7. Ibid., arts. 156, 166, 169, and 170.
8. Ibid., arts. 171; and 189, no. 6.
9. Ibid., art. 189, no. 10.
10. Ibid., art. 173.
11. Ibid., art. 159.
12. Ibid., art. 173.
13. Ibid.
14. Ibid., arts. 174 and 175.
15. Ibid., art. 176.
16. Ibid., art. 177.
17. Ibid., art. 178.
18. Ibid., art. 177.

19. Ibid., arts. 172 and 246.
20. Ibid., arts. 170, nos. 6 and 14; and 189, no. 12.
21. Ibid., art. 170, no. 13.
22. Ibid., art. 170, no. 14.
23. Ibid., arts. 172 and 246.
24. Ibid., art. 170, nos. 13 and 14.
25. Ibid., art. 181.
26. Ibid., art. 189, no. 4.
27. Ibid.
28. Ibid.

haiti

1. Constitution

2. Decree [with Force of Law] Law Treaties [Legislative] Decree

3. Order (Arrêté)

CONSTITUTION (Constitution). The supremacy of the charter is established in the constitutional passage which provides that the law may not add to or delete from the constitutional text; the text of the charter shall always prevail. Control of the constitutionality of the laws is entrusted to the Court of Cassation which decides when the application of a law is in question.[1]

The constitution may be amended provided that a declaration is issued by the legislature stating the need to revise the charter partially or totally. This statement should be made to the president of the republic and published in the official daily. Thereafter, the *Corps Legislatif,* or Legislative Chamber, meets as a National Assembly to consider and rule on the proposed revision which, once completed, is proclaimed, in a special session by the National Assembly, as the new constitution or amendments thereto.[2] The constitution currently in force was enacted in 1964, as amended by a 1971 decree issued by the National Assembly. No other amendments were found since 1971 in the available sources.

Contradictory to the constitutional precept that the executive, legislative, and judicial powers are independent from one another and may not delegate their assigned functions or trespass each other's limits,[3] each year the Haitian legislature issues a legislative decree suspending a number of constitutional provisions, among these the separation of powers, the legality of administrative acts, restrictions to the presidential powers, and procedures for amending the constitution. Furthermore, it grants the *président à vie* (president for life) extraordinary powers to legislate by means of decrees with force of law for the preservation of the integrity of the national territory, the sovereignty of the state, the consolidation of order and peace, the maintenance of economic and financial stability, and the fostering of the welfare of the rural and urban population in defense of the general interests of the republic. Although the supremacy of the constitution has not been expressly or directly challenged, the delegation of extraordinary powers is limitless. This suggests that in actuality the decrees issued by the president under these circumstances may at times rank as high as the constitution itself.

LOI (Law). Under the Haitian charter, legislative power is vested in the Legislative Chamber, a single body, which is entrusted with the responsibilities of enacting laws on matters of general interest.[4] Bills, except those covering public expenditures, pensions, bonuses, subsidies, or allotments, which are the sole prerogative of the president, may be submitted either by the Legislative Chamber or by the executive branch.[5]

Bills must be considered and voted upon provision by provision and then voted upon in their entirety. Decisions to enact are made by a majority vote of the members attending the corresponding session.[6] Once the law is passed by the chamber, it is forwarded to the president of the republic who may veto it, either partially or totally, within eight days.[7] The chamber may insist on its original position with a two-thirds vote. Should the chamber fail to do so, executive objections shall stand as stated.[8]

Laws enacted by this process are promulgated by the executive branch.[9] Examination of the official daily, *Le Moniteur,* indicates that this promulgation is performed in the text of the same instrument which contains the text of the law. A law appears under the heading *loi* followed by an introductory statement justifying its issuance. The text of the provisions appears next and is then followed by the order of the president for the great seal of the republic, the printing, the publishing, and the execution thereof. The instrument is signed by the president and countersigned by all the secretaries of the cabinet. It is not certain whether all laws are processed in this manner or not. The only samples found for examination were laws originally proposed by the president after deliberation with the Council of the Secretaries of State (cabinet members). The constitution does not include any provisions on this subject. Laws originally proposed by the Legislative Chamber may or may not conform to the above procedural pattern and format.

Laws become official and enforceable by being published in the official daily. They are inserted in a bulletin entitled *Bulletin des Lois et Actes.* Nevertheless, the date officially assigned to the law is that of its definitive enactment by the Legislative Chamber.[10]

DECRET [LEGISLATIF] ([Legislative] Decree). This is an instrument only indirectly referred to by the constitution. The pertinent passage states that the president shall be responsible for the enforcement of the constitution and the laws, acts, and decrees of the legislative body and the National Assembly.[11]

Only a few samples of decrees were found in the official gazette. They show that decrees originate in the Legislative Chamber and, except for the heading, their content and format are similar to those of laws. They are promulgated by the president of the republic supported by all the secretaries of his cabinet. Finally, they are also published in the official gazette.

The only written source available in the Library of Congress states that usage of decrees has changed and that presently the designation applies mostly to the decisions issued by the National Assembly or to acts of provisional governments.[12]

No reference to the authority rank of the decrees has been found in the constitution or elsewhere. No monographic material was available either.

TRAITÉ INTERNATIONAL (International Treaty). Negotiation and completion of international treaties and agreements are entrusted to the president of the republic, but their enforcement in Haiti still requires the approval of the National Assembly.[13]

The constitution does not indicate whether or not a specific type of instrument is required for such approval by the National Assembly. Examination of legislative indexes and corresponding issues of the official daily over a ten-year period produced no evidence that such an instrument had ever been issued.

It was discovered, however, that all international treaties and related instruments have been approved by decrees issued by the president of the republic in pursuance of the legislative decrees granting him full powers.

As to authority rank of the international treaties and agreements, no reference was found in the constitution or the general literature, except for the statement that the constitution shall always prevail over all other forms of legislative instruments.[14] Their relationship with other legislative instruments is therefore uncertain.

DECRET [AYANT FORCE DE LOIS] (Decree [with Force of Law]). In the last ten years Haiti has established the practice of granting the president of the republic a concentration of special powers as stated in the constitution. He exercises these extraordinary powers through the issuance of decrees which are given the force of laws. Matters covered by decrees apparently are not limited.

These instruments do not have a specific subheading or number to differentiate them from the decrees issued by the ordinary Legislative Chamber. The careful reader can identify them by the references to and quotations from the corresponding legislative decree from which the president derives the powers for issuance.

The authority ranking of these instruments is not completely clear. The matters covered suggest they are at least equivalent in strength to the laws. However, considering that constitutional provisions controlling amendments thereto are suspended, it may very well be that the president could even amend the constitution by means of a decree with force of law.

ARRÊTÉ (Executive Decree or Order). This is an instrument issued by the president of the republic, who has executive power and discharges his responsibilities with the support of one secretary of the cabinet or all of them acting as the Council of Ministers.[15] The charter grants him the power to issue regulations and *arrêtés* to enforce the constitution and all legislative issuances of the National Assembly. He is also empowered to issue these instruments when the National Assembly is dissolved so that public services can be properly administered.[16]

Legislative indexes and the official daily revealed that presidential power is exercised through the *arrêté.* Evidence of such other instruments as the regulation was not found. In some cases, however, decrees issued by the executive under special presidential powers did contain regulatory material.

Notes

1. *Constitution* (1964, as Amended in 1971) (Washington, D.C.: Organization of American States, 1974), arts. 38 and 121; also published in *Le Moniteur* (January 20, 1971).
2. *Const.*, arts. 198 and 199.
3. Ibid., art. 48.
4. Ibid., art. 49.
5. Ibid., arts. 68 and 151.

6. Ibid., arts. 74, 75, and 76.
7. Ibid., arts. 78 and 80.
8. Ibid., art. 79.
9. Ibid., arts. 78, 79, 81, and 93.
10. Ibid., arts. 83, 84, and 196.
11. Ibid., art. 93.
12. H. Price, *Dictionnaire de Législation Administrative Haitienne,* 10th ed. (Port-au-Prince: Imprimerie CHERAQUIT, 1923), p. 100.
13. *Const.,* arts. 56, no. 2; and 93.
14. Ibid., art. 38.
15. Ibid., arts. 90, 94, 99 to 104, and 106.
16. Ibid., arts. 93 and 62.

honduras

Under the Constitution

1. Constitution

2. Treaties   [Legislative] Decree

3. (Executive) Decree   Accord

Current Status

1. Constitution   Decree Law   Decree

2. Treaties

3. Accord

honduras

CONSTITUCIÓN (Constitution). Constitutional supremacy is not expressly established by the charter, but a number of provisions imply this supremacy by requiring subordination or conformity to the charter.[1] Broadly speaking, laws that either deviate from or oppose the constitution may be challenged before the Supreme Court by the parties directly affected. The high tribunal considers individual cases and decides whether or not the allegations of unconstitutionality are legally grounded. The court's decision, does not have a general character[2] and only benefits the parties involved.

The constitution currently in force was enacted by a National Constituent Assembly on June 3, 1965, to take effect on June 6 of that year.[3] It was reaffirmed with serious limitations by a decree issued by the chief of state on December 6, 1972. The executive decree ordered that the constitution remain in force only as far as it did not oppose the provisions issued by the government in power.[4]

The charter provides that amendments thereto be introduced in resolutions issued by two consecutive congresses. The first resolution must state the content and scope of the amendment, while the second resolution ratifies the amendment.[5] Examination of a number of issues of the Honduran official gazette indicates that the National Congress exercises its power through an instrument called a decree which contains congressional resolutions. The amendatory decrees are published in the official gazette, *La Gaceta.*

Constitutional provisions concerning the form of government, the term of office of the president and his reeligibility or noneligibility, for the executive office, and amendatory procedures applicable to the charter may not be amended.[6]

Current Status. Pres. Oswaldo López, who seized power through a coup, was ousted by the military on April 23, 1975. The military apparently did not overrule the former government's legislative issuances concerning the organization and functioning of the powers of the state. The present government has also followed the legislative practices established by its predecessor and is governing through decree laws and decrees, instruments issued by the president alone or in conjunction with his Council of Ministers. These instruments may oppose or amend the constitution. A recent decree reaffirms this assertion by establishing the Advisory Council to the chief of state, which is in charge of drafting an electoral statute for the government.[7] The stated intention for establishing this council was to prepare the country for a return to the rule of law under a constitution. No evidence was found that the promised statute was enacted.

DECRETO [LEGISLATIVO] ([Legislative] Decree). Concerning the rank of laws, it is believed that they are subordinate to the charter based on constitutional statements implying supremacy.[8] Legislating is entrusted to a Congress of Deputies which has the power to enact, interpret, amend, and repeal laws. Procedural norms for the issuance of legislǎtive instruments are provided by the constitution. The general context of the provisions are designated laws.[9] However, the instrument containing the laws used by Congress in the exercise of its legislative powers is designated as a decree. Considerable examination of issues of the official gazette revealed that sometimes these decrees bear a subheading worded, "law on . . ." followed by the subject covered. The constitution does not state that specific matters require the use of this subheading, nor did the gazettes reveal any system for the assignment of the subheading, except when the content of the decree is a systematic body of provisions on a specific subject.

Bills to be enacted in this category may be introduced by the deputies of Congress and the president of the republic through the secretary of state, and the Supreme Court on matters of their competence.[10] Bills must be debated in three separate sessions before a vote is taken, unless Congress declares them urgent.[11] Bills with passages affecting the codes of the republic may be debated only after the opinion of the Supreme Court is heard.[12] When a bill affects an autonomous agency, the opinion of this agency must also be heard.[13]

Instruments approved by Congress are forwarded to the president of the republic who may sanction them into law or object to them with a veto. If the veto is based on unconstitutionality, the Supreme Court is required to give an opinion before the objection is submitted to congressional consideration. If by a two-thirds vote of the legislature the bill retains its original nature, it shall be returned to the president for publication as a law.[14] The pertinent passages of the charter concerning the proportion of votes is ambiguous, and there is presently no literature available on the topic. Questions remain unanswered: Is the proportion of votes in Congress calculated on the attending members only or the total membership of the legislature? Is the proportion of votes prescribed to override the presidential veto also valid for approval of a bill?

The charter entrused certain functions exclusively to the National Congress, which include personnel appointments, acceptance of resignations, decrees related to the conduct of the executive power, the budget law, and treaties and contracts disapproved by Congress.[15] Actions resulting from these functions are specifically excluded from the threat of a presidential veto.

Enactments sanctioned by the president may be identified by the closing statement, "be it therefore executed." Instruments not sanctioned by the chief executive simply bear the statement, "be it therefore published." The promulgation of decrees is performed by the president of the republic and the corresponding cabinet minister or ministers.[16]

A law is enforceable by virtue of its promulgation, twenty days after its publication in the official daily, but this period can be reduced or extended. Other forms of promulgation may be ordered under special circumstances.[17]

Current Status. As stated, the current government seems to have adopted the rules and practices of the former regime. A perusal of the text of decrees issued by the current chief of state reveals that the source of authority he claims is Decree no. 1 of December 6, 1972. This instrument, however, has no apparent provisions covering the issuance of legislative instruments or the manner in which the responsibilities assigned shall be discharged.

Copies of the official newspaper reveal that the government has been fulfilling its legislative duties by issuing both decrees and decree laws signed by the president of the republic and countersigned by all the ministers of the cabinet. No difference has been found in their subject or format. For example, both decrees and decree laws have exempted imports for commercial firms from custom duties, or approved and ratified international treaties and agreements. It is possible that a decree may amend a decree law and vice versa.

TRATADO INTERNACIONAL (International Treaty). The president of the republic is vested by the charter with the power to conclude treaties with foreign powers.[18] These instruments require approval by Congress under the same procedural norms prescribed for all other congressional instruments,[19] except that this congressional approval cannot be challenged by the presidential veto, nor does it require sanctioning by the president.[20]

No provisions were found in the constitution assigning authority rank to international treaties and agreements within the Honduran legal system. Under the assumption that the constitution is supreme, we conclude that international instruments are at least subordinate to the charter.

Current Status. An examination of the official gazette indicates that international treaties and agreements are drawn up at the initiative of the chief executive. In practice, they are approved by decree law, decree, or *acuerdo* (accord).

DECRETO (Decree). The charter expressly provides that none of the acts exercised by the executive power may oppose the content of laws.[21] This power is entrusted to the president of the republic or one of his designates. Issuances resulting from the exercise of this power must be signed by the president and countersigned by one or more of his cabinet ministers. The cabinet may assist the president, in which case it is designated the Council of Ministers.[22]

The constitution refers to decrees, regulations, accords, and *providencias* (orders and instructions) as instruments issued within the competence of the chief executive. Some sources indicate that the president issued regulations and other legislative instruments by means of decrees while the constitution was still in full force. All decrees bore the signatures of the president and all his ministers of the cabinet, acting as the Council of State.

The only expressed delegation of congressional legislative power to the president is the issuing of decrees during congressional recess for expenses when funds are insufficient or have not been budgeted. These decrees shall, however, be submitted to Congress as soon as possible.[23] Finally, all decrees are published in *La Gaceta.*

Current Status. Examination of indexes and copies of the official gazette show that decrees from the executive are not issued currently.

ACUERDO (Accord). There are no direct references to the authority rank of this instrument in the charter or in the related statutes and literature. Available sources state that accords were once issued under varying circumstances and with differing content. Under the constitution and when there still was a Congress, accords were apparently reserved for such administrative matters as exempting couples from the legal obligation of publishing matrimonial banns as a marriage requirement.

Current Status. The content of current accords was previously assigned only to decrees. Accords are all signed by the president and one or more ministers of the cabinet, but no accords were found signed by the Council of Ministers. Accords are always published in the official gazette.

Notes

1. Decree no. 20 of the National Constituent Assembly of June 3, 1965, arts. 230, no. 11, and 234 to 237, *La Gaceta* (*L.G.*) (June 12, 1965); amended by Decree no. 130 of the National Congress of February 5, 1971, *L.G.* (March 18, 1971); ratified by Decree no. 2 of the National Congress of May 28, 1971, *L.G.* (June 2, 1971).
2. Ibid., art. 237.
3. Ibid., art. 347.
4. Decree no. 1 of December 6, 1972, *L.G.* (December 7, 1972).
5. Ibid., art. 342.
6. Ibid., arts. 4, 192, 193, 196, and 342.
7. Decree no. 327 of March 9, 1976, *L.G.* (March 11, 1976).
8. *Constitución de la República, Decreto número 20 de la Asamblea Nacional Constituyente*, 1965, *L.G.* (June 12, 1965), art. 234.
9. Ibid., art. 245.
10. Ibid., arts. 239; and 201, no. 32.
11. Ibid., art. 240.
12. Ibid., art. 246.
13. Ibid., art. 307.
14. Ibid., arts. 241 and 243.
15. Ibid., art. 245.
16. Ibid., arts. 241; 245; 201, no. 33; and 203.
17. Ibid., art. 248.
18. Ibid., art. 201, no. 26.
19. Ibid., art. 181, no. 26.
20. Ibid., art. 245, no. 7.
21. Ibid., art. 201, no. 35.
22. Ibid., arts. 190, 203, and 207.
23. Ibid., art. 285.

MEXICO

1. Constitution
2. Law (Legislative) Decree Treaties
3. Regulation [Executive] Decree Accord

CONSTITUCION (Constitution). The supremacy of the Mexican charter was established when a constituent congress enacted a constitution on January 31, 1917. It took effect on May 1 of that year,[1] and has been amended several times since. The pertinent passage states that the constitution, the laws enacted by the Mexican National Congress, and all treaties with foreign powers concluded in pursuance thereof by the president of the republic with the approval of the Senate are the supreme law of the Union of Mexican States.[2] Despite the apparent equality of the instruments, the supremacy of the charter is reaffirmed by the provision which states that laws and international treaties may not contradict the constitution.[3]

Amendments to the constitution may only be introduced by the National Congress by a two-thirds vote of the attending membership. It is further required that the amendment be approved by the majority of the legislatures of the Mexican states.[4] Theoretically, the president is vested with power to veto all legislative enactments; nevertheless, there are serious discrepancies concerning the exercise of this power vis-à-vis constitutional amendments. A noted Mexican scholar stated that the word *law* (*ley*) has a broad meaning encompassing the laws and the constitution as well. Apparently in practice constitutional amendments may be subject to presidential vetoes.[5] Constitutional amendments are contained in decrees which will be described in the following section.[6]

LEY, DECRETO (Law, Decree). The legislative power is vested in a general Congress consisting of two chambers, the House and the Senate.[7] The legislative process takes place in this Congress, but it is completed by the executive in the office of the president of the republic.[8] There are exceptional circumstances in which the president of the republic may issue laws by himself, either by delegation of the corresponding congressional powers, or by direct authorization granted by the constitution.[9]

According to the constitutional text, a congressional legislative decision takes the form of either a law or a decree.[10] No distinction in content or format exists in the constitution between these basic instruments. A well-known author states that the distinction existed in the past. Laws contained provisions of general concern, and decrees controled matters of an individual character.[11] At present, laws and decrees coexist at the same level of hierarchy. They may amend or repeal one another with no apparent dominance of one over the other. The procedural norms controlling their enactment are identical.

Bills may be submitted to Congress by its members, the state legislatures, and the president of the republic.[12] Debates may be initiated in either congressional chamber except when the bill submitted is related to public debt, taxation, importation or the induction of troops, in which cases debates must first be held at the Chamber of Deputies. The passage of a law or a decree requires that both congressional bodies debate upon and approve the bill by a majority vote of the attending members. Once approved, the instrument is forwarded to the president of the republic who may either approve or veto it. If the latter occurs, the vetoed bill is sent back to Congress for further debate. If the bill is reaffirmed in its original form by a two-thirds vote of both chambers, it becomes a law or a congressional decree and is forwarded to the president who must comply with the formal requirement of promulgation.[13]

According to a scholar, the term promulgation, within the context of the Mexican constitution, is equivalent to publication.[14] To discharge this responsibility, the president issues an executive decree which carries the text of the congressional instrument, that is a law or a legislative decree. Examination of a reasonable number of issues of the Mexican official gazette showed that these instruments are not identified by a number or any other denomination.

Instruments of congressional origin are not listed separately in the table of contents of the gazette; they are included with the simple decrees of executive issuance and their congressional nature is not indicated. All instruments published by the official gazette are therefore exclusively executive in origin, a confusing practice for a reader unfamiliar with Mexican legal sources.

Laws or decrees take effect three days after their publication in the official gazette, unless otherwise stated by the instruments themselves. This term is extended according to the distance a given location is from the instrument's place of publication, one day for each forty kilometers.[15]

Laws and legislative decrees are ranked at the same level directly under the constitution.[16]

TRATADO INTERNACIONAL (International Treaty). According to a previously cited passage of the constitution, treaties entered into with foreign powers are the supreme law of the nation along with the constitution and the laws.[17] Nevertheless, and as indicated by a legal scholar, international treaties and agreements are undoubtedly subordinated to the constitution.[18] There are no references in the constitution or in other legal sources to the hierarchical relationship between international treaties and congressional laws or decrees.

International treaties and agreements are negotiated by the president of the republic.[19] Enforcement thereof however is subject to approval by the Senate which proceeds to do so by means of a decree.[20] Ratification of the instrument by the president is an additional requirement. This formality is complied with through the issuance of another executive decree, signed by the chief executive and the secretary of foreign affairs. An apparent contradiction concerning this matter exists in the charter. The pertinent passage states that approval of international treaties is a matter entrusted to the federal Congress.[21] Another related passage assigned this power to only one of the legislative bodies, the Senate.[22] The author consulted on this topic asserted that the contradiction has been resolved by assigning this responsibility to the Senate only in accordance with the more specific constitutional statement.[23]

Traditionally, approved international treaties are published in the official gazette as an integral part of the ratifying executive decree.

REGLAMENTO (Regulation or Regulatory Executive Decree). The powers granted to the executive branch are exercised by the president of the republic.[24] One of the instruments by means of which the president performs his duties is the regulation.[25] The chief executive is also empowered to issue *decretos* (decrees), and *órdenes* (executive orders). These instruments must be signed by the president and countersigned by the corresponding secretary of the cabinet before they can take effect.[26]

The regulation is a body of general provisions issued to implement the even more general provisions of a previous law. No regulation may be issued unless there is a previous law requiring such implementation. Regulations are therefore subordinate to their original legal source which they may not amend or repeal.[27] They may be published in the official gazette and are subject to the same formalities as are prescribed for the laws to be enforced.[28]

DECRETO ([Executive] Decree). Neither the charter nor any other related sources discuss the differences between this instrument and the regulation. A perusal of instruments in this category found in a number of issues of the official gazette indicated that, by and large, executive decrees are used to promulgate congressional decrees. Nevertheless, there were instances when an executive decree was also issued to establish a public agency or to legislate on such matters as taxation.

No sources, statutory or otherwise, were found that defined the executive decree in theory or practice. Nor were references found on their hierarchy in the scheme of Mexican legal instruments, except for the formality of publication previously mentioned.

ACUERDO (Accord). This is another instrument of executive issuance. Its content may cover a wide variety of subjects, such as granting bonuses to federal employees, transfering property rights to a certain entity, or forfeiting concessionary rights. We have been unable to ascertain which matters are covered in practice by this instrument.

Concerning the hierarchical rank of the accord within the system, it is apparent that it must conform to the laws and congressional decrees. No references were found concerning the hierarchical relationship between the accord, the executive decree, and the regulation.

Notes

1. *Constitución política mexicana* (containing the constitutional text in force as of February 26, 1977) (Mexico, D.F.: Ediciones Andrade, S.A., 1969); for the English version, see *Constitution of Mexico 1917, as Amended* (Washington, D.C.: Organization of American States, 1972) (hereafter cited as *Const.*).
2. Ibid., art. 133.

3. Ibid., arts. 107 and 15; I. Burgoa, *Derecho constitutional mexicano*, 2d ed. (Mexico: Editorial Porrúa S.A., 1976), p. 348 (hereafter cited as Burgoa, *Derecho*); G. Fraga, *Derecho administrativo*, 16th ed. (Mexico: Editorial Porrúa S.A., 1975), p. 40 (hereafter cited as Fraga, *Derecho*).

4. *Const.*, art. 135.

5. Burgoa, *Derecho*, p. 729.

6. Fraga, *Derecho*, p. 41.

7. *Const.*, art. 50.

8. Ibid., arts. 65, III; 71; and 73, XXX.

9. Ibid., arts. 49; and 27, V; Burgoa, *Derecho*, p. 726.

10. *Const.*, art. 70.

11. Fraga, *Derecho*, p. 38.

12. *Const.*, art. 71.

13. Ibid., art. 72.

14. Burgoa, *Derecho*, p. 730.

15. *Código Civil para el Distrito Federal*, 39th ed., arts. 3, 4, and 6c (Mexico, D.F.: Editorial Porrúa, S.A., 1975) (hereafter cited as *C. Civ.*).

16. *Const.*, art. 107, VIIIa); Burgoa, *Derecho*, p. 348; Fraga, *Derecho*, p. 40.

17. *Const.*, art. 33.

18. Burgoa, *Derecho*, p. 348.

19. *Const.*, art. 89, X.

20. Ibid., art. 76, I.

21. Ibid., art. 89, X.

22. Ibid., art. 76, I.

23. Burgoa, *Derecho*, p. 659.

24. *Const.*, art. 80.

25. Ibid., art. 89, I.

26. Ibid., art. 92.

27. Burgoa, *Derecho*, p. 732.

28. *C. Civ.*, art. 3.

NICARAGUA

1. Constitution
2. Constitutional Law
3. Decree Law [Legislative] Decree [Legislative] Resolution Treaties
4. Regulation [Executive] Decree Accord

CONSTITUCIÓN (Constitution). According to the fundamental provisions of the Nicaraguan charter, the constitution is the supreme law of the land. Any laws, decrees, regulations, executive orders, ordinances, pacts, international treaties, and agreements must conform thereto.[1] This principle is reaffirmed by the provision which states that courts and judges of the republic shall base their decisions first on the constitution and constitutional laws, then on the laws and decrees, and lastly on the executive decrees and accords.[2] The control of constitutional conformity of all legislative acts is entrusted to the Supreme Court of the republic.[3]

Amendments to the constitution may either be total or partial.[4] Proposals for partial amendments must be submitted to the Chamber of Deputies, one of the two legislative bodies, with the supporting signatures of at least fifteen chamber members. The rather elaborate processing of the proposal is spelled out in detail in the charter. Similar procedural steps are followed in the Senate. If both legislative bodies agree, a joint draft is submitted for debating and voting upon. Approval of the draft requires the favorable vote of the majority of the members present at the joint session. After approval, the instrument is forwarded to the president of the republic for approval or veto. In cases of either partial or total veto of a constitutional amendment, further joint legislative debates are required.[5] Amendments to the constitutional provisions concerning reelection of the president of the republic or election to that office of an immediate relative of the incumbent for the ensuing presidential term do not take effect during the term the amendment is enacted or in the subsequent one.[6] The pertinent passage of the charter does not refer to the presidential term explicitly, but the general context of the document makes it rather obvious that this is the only logical interpretation.

Total amendment of the constitution may not occur until after ten years from the date of its enactment. A proposal of this nature requires that Congress issue an instrument stating that this amendment is viable. A national constituent assembly is then elected to consider and debate the draft submitted to it by the drafting commission also appointed ad hoc by Congress.[7] The role of the president of the republic in the amendatory process was not discussed in the charter or related sources.[8] The legislature goes into recess while the constituent assembly is active.

The current Nicaraguan charter was enacted by a constituent assembly on March 14, 1974, and took effect on April 24, the day of its publication in the national official gazette.

LEY CONSTITUCIONAL (Constitutional Law). This instrument is assigned the same rank as the constitution[9] and consists of a limited category of statutes. They are specified in the charter as follows: the law of amparo, martial law, and electoral law.[10] A national author provides the rationale for this equivalence by stating that these statutes are direct supplements to the constitutional text.[11]

No provisions in the constitution indicated any special procedure for the enactment of these constitutional statutes. Examination of the current statutes in this category showed that they were enacted by a constituent assembly.[12] It was also found that other legislative issuances of the same body were not related to this category.[13] The format of constitutional laws is identical to that of ordinary laws, selected aspects of which are discussed below.

DECRETO [LEGISLATIVO], RESOLUCIÓN; ([Legislative] Decree, Resolution). The exercise of legislative power is basically entrusted to the Nicaraguan Congress which consists of two bodies, the Chamber of Deputies and the Senate.[14] The activities resulting from this exercise of power are enacting, amending, interpreting, and repealing laws.[15] The constitution devotes an entire chapter to the legal process.[16] However, examination of the related passages revealed that in fact there is no specific instrument identified under the heading law which is used to enact legislative issuances. Apparently, a legislative issuance is simply entitled a [legislative] decree. Other congressional decisions known as resolutions (*resoluciones*) and legislative statements (*declaraciones legislativas*) are also not identified under the denomination law.

All these legislative instruments may be submitted to the Chamber of Deputies by its members[17] or by the executive, provided the drafts are presented through the corresponding minister of the cabinet.[18] The Supreme Court may submit bills which are related to the administration of justice. The same is provided by the charter with regard to the Electoral Tribunal.[19] Such bills as pensions, temporary privileges, subsidies, and transfer of state property may only be submitted to the legislature at the exclusive initiative of the executive.[20]

Bills are debated upon by both chambers of the legislature and their decisions, by and large, are adopted by a majority vote of the attending members.[21] Exceptions are explicitly stated in the charter. Bills concerning amendments to the civil, criminal, and commercial codes and their corresponding codes of procedure may not be subject to congressional debate without previously consulting the Supreme Court. This formality can only be waived if the Supreme Court fails to act within the prescribed term.[22]

Once the bill is approved by both the Chamber of Deputies and the Senate, the instrument is forwarded to the executive for approval or veto within ten days.[23] If vetoed, the bill is returned to Congress for further debate in joint legislative sessions of the two houses. Congress may override the veto and reaffirm its original stand by a two-thirds vote of the attending members. The same proportion of votes is required to approve presidential objections. Once the legislature either reaffirms itself or accepts the presidential objections, the bill is returned to the president for promulgation.[24]

The budget law and a few others which do not require presidential promulgation are simply published in the official gazette.[25] Promulgations by the executive must take place within ten days. If this is not accomplished, the president of the Congress shall do so by virtue of the power vested in him by the charter under such circumstances.[26] The requirement of publication is met by insertion of the corresponding texts in the official gazette and the laws are enforceable throughout the national territory thirty days after being published. Any exception to this term must be explicitly provided for in the corresponding instrument.[27]

The legislative decree, when containing the text of a law, will very likely display a subheading indicating this content. Nevertheless, examination of issues of the official gazette showed that sometimes legislative decrees may carry material typically assigned to the law category, but no reference is made to this effect. Finally, the legal literature on these legislative issuances may simply designate these instruments as laws or *leyes,* or as legislative decrees. To avoid confusion, the English-speaking reader must exercise caution when searching Nicaraguan material in this category.

Legislative decrees are published as insertions in another instrument issued by the president of the republic as part of his duty to promulgate. This presidential instrument displays no heading, only a closing paragraph stating that the preceding text of law, decree, resolution, or legislative statement "be it executed" or "be it published," depending on the type of instrument concerned, and the role of the executive assigned thereon.[28]

Concerning hierarchy, laws are directly subordinate to the constitution and the constitutional laws.[29] No references were found concerning the rank of the other instruments of legislative issuance referred to above.

The general principle that the major legislative role should be entrusted to Congress has some exceptions. For example, the charter allows Congress to delegate its legislative powers to the executive on certain specific subject matters while the former is in recess.[30] The same situation develops when there is a need for a total constitutional amendment and a constituent assembly is established. In this case, Congress is adjourned to make room for the assembly. The executive branch assumes the orindary legislative powers needed to maintain legal control for the duration of the assembly's assignment.[31] The president of the republic is then supposed to issue laws under these circumstances,[32] but no examples of such issuances were found in the available sources.

Under extraordinary circumstances, the president of the republic may also assume full legislative powers and issue another type of instrument, the decree law, which will be discussed in some detail below.

RESOLUCIÓN (Resolution). This is another instrument resulting from the exercise of congressional legislative powers. Neither the constitution nor any other available sources on the topic describe differences that may exist between the resolution and other congressional issuances. The official gazette revealed that Congress has used this instrument for the approval of international treaties and agreements.

Procedural steps for enactment of congressional resolutions are the same as those for congressional decrees.[33] No references were found concerning the hierarchical ranking of the resolution within the Nicaraguan legal system except the general principle of constitutional supremacy, that is, ultimate subordination to the charter.[34]

TRATADO INTERNACIONAL (International Treaty). The negotiation of these instruments is entrusted to the executive. Completion of negotiations by the president of the republic with a foreign power is marked by the issuance of an executive instrument designated *acuerdo,* or accord, approving the treaty or agreement and submitting it to Congress for further approval.[35] Once the latter formality has been complied with, the document returns to the president of the republic for formal ratification. Congressional approval is issued in a resolution; presidential ratification is done by a [executive] decree bearing the signatures of the president and the corresponding minister of the cabinet.

No statutes concerned themselves with the ranking of international treaties and agreements within the system. Nevertheless, a Nicaraguan author has reported that parity between international treaties and law has been accepted.[36] Consequently, predominance of one over the other is a simple question of chronology. The instrument of more recent enactment prevails over the superseded one, unless otherwise indicated in the original treaty.

All three instruments needed to put an international treaty or agreement into force are published separately as is the text of the treaty.

DECRETO-LEY (Decree Law). The president of the republic, together with the Council of Ministers, may issue decree laws, in cases of emergency and urgent public necessity, provided Congress is in recess.[37] This instrument has the format of a decree, but its content is that of a law. Despite its authority and seriousness, there are no apparent statutory provisions prescribing any procedural norms to be observed for its issuance.

A decree law shares the same rank as an ordinary law of congressional origin.[38]

REGLAMENTO (Regulation). The exercise of executive power by the president of the republic may require the support of one of his cabinet ministers or all of them as a body in a council.[39] Since one of his basic responsibilities is to implement the laws, the president does so by issuing the *reglamento,* or regulation, which may not violate or distort the laws from which it originates.[40] Its authority rank is, therefore, subordinate to the law, congressional resolution, and decree law. As is the case of most instruments, there are no references to the hierarchical relationships between this and other instruments issued by the executive, except in the case of the decree law.

DECRETO, ACUERDO [EJECUTIVO] ([Executive] Decree, Accord). Other duties performed by the president of the republic are channeled through decrees or accords. Both instruments have rather poor written coverage, a circumstance which, together with broad generalizations in the charter on the topic, makes the task of describing either format or content almost impossible. The only clues are the samples examined in the few issues of the official gazette where this category of instrument was published. Both decrees and accords are issued under the signatures of the president of the republic and the corresponding minister of the cabinet. Their subject matter was observed to vary. As to rank, the charter places these instruments under the ordinary laws and decree laws.[41]

Notes

1. *Constitución política* [of March 14, 1974], *La Gaceta* (*L.G.*) (March 24, 1974): art. 332 (hereafter cited as *Const.*).
2. Ibid., art. 311.
3. Ibid., art. 293, no. 8.
4. Ibid., art. 334.
5. Ibid., art. 335.
6. Ibid., art. 338.
7. Ibid., art. 336.
8. Ibid., art. 337.
9. Ibid., art. 311.
10. Ibid., art. 331.
11. M. Escobar H., *Derecho constitucional nicaragüense*, 2d ed. (Masaya, Nicaragua: Talleres Tipográficos "El Espectador," 1951), p. 6.
12. *Ley de amparo* [of October 25, 1974], *L.G.* (November 11, 1974); *Ley marcial* [of October 25, 1974], *L.G.* (November 11, 1974).
13. As an example, decree no. 428 which regulates the extradition procedure, in *L.G.* (September 2, 1974).
14. *Const.*, art. 127.
15. Ibid., art. 148, 1.
16. Ibid., arts. 161 to 179.
17. Ibid., art. 162.
18. Ibid., arts. 161; and 190, 6.
19. Ibid., arts. 161; and 293, 9.
20. Ibid., arts. 149; and 190, 4.
21. Ibid., art. 134.
22. Ibid., art. 178.
23. Ibid., arts. 169 to 171; and 190, 7.
24. Ibid., arts. 160, 8; 190, 7; 170; and 171.
25. Ibid., arts. 175; 190, 8; and 226.
26. Ibid., art. 174.
27. *Código Civil*, 3rd official ed. (Managua: Casa Editorial Carlos Heuberger y Cia., 1931), I: tit. prel. I, I and II.
28. *Const.*, art. 191.
29. Ibid., art. 311.
30. Ibid., art. 150.
31. Ibid., art. 336.
32. Ibid., art. 190, 9.
33. Ibid., art. 161.
34. Ibid., art. 332.
35. Ibid., arts 190, 6; 148, 8; and 194, 8 and 9.
36. A. Montiel Argüello, *Manual de derecho internacional* (Managua, 1969), p. 8, n. 1.
37. *Const.*, art. 190, 10.
38. Ibid., art. 311.
39. Ibid., arts. 179 and 200.
40. Ibid., art. 194, 3.
41. Ibid., art. 311.

panama

1. Constitution

2. Treaties

3. Law

4. Decree Resolution

CONSTITUCIÓN (Constitution). Constitutional prevalence over all other legislative instruments is derived from the constitutional provision establishing that the Supreme Court shall decide all cases concerning the constitutionality of laws, decrees, accords, resolutions, and other acts. The court's decisions are final and published in the official gazette.[1] The constitution currently in force was decreed by the National Constituent Assembly on October 11, 1972, and came into force on November 11 of the same year.[2]

Amendments to the charter may be introduced by the National Council of Legislation to the National Assembly of Representatives of *Corregimientos,* the basic Panamanian geopolitical unit which is comparable to a county. Both political bodies perform the legislative functions.[3] Only a majority vote is required for approval of an amendment. After first approval, if the term has begun, the instrument requires additional approval by the National Assembly of Representatives elected for the subsequent term.[4]

Amendments to the charter are published in the official gazette within six days from the date of their enactment.[5] Sources consulted do not designate the instrument through which constitutional amendments are enacted.

TRATADO INTERNACIONAL (International Treaty). The president of the republic is entrusted with the power to negotiate treaties and agreements with foreign powers.[6] However, these instruments also require submission to and approval by the representatives' Assembly for enactment and enforcement. The Assembly may not introduce amendments to treaties; its functions are confined to their approval or disapproval.[7] Approval is accomplished by means of a law enacted by the Assembly.[8]

The charter currently in force has granted extraordinary powers to Brig. Gen. Omar Torrijos, commander in chief of the national guard, to conduct the foreign relations of Panama and other business for six years.[9]

The current Panamanian constitution has also conferred upon General Torrijos, designated the "maximum leader of the Panamanian revolution," the following special and extraordinary powers: coordinating the task of public administration, appointing and dismissing all high government officials as well as the chief commanders and officers of the public forces, appointing justices of the Supreme Court and the attorney general, and negotiating loans and public contracts. General Torrijos is also a participating and voting member of the Cabinet Council, the National Legislative Council, the National Assembly of Representatives of *Corregimientos,* the Provincial Coordinating Council, and the Municipal Juntas. These entities represent the top-level political decision-making bodies of Panama.

Returning to the legal instrument of the international treaty, there are special treaty provisions for the Panama Canal, its adjacent zones, their protection, and the construction of a third set of locks. Treaties and agreements on these matters require submission to and acceptance by a national plebiscite.[10]

There are no specific provisions in the charter regarding the hierarchy of international instruments. Nevertheless, a Panamanian scholar stated that although treaties and agreements are laws in the formal sense, in fact they have a special status. They may not be repealed in Panama by subsequent ordinary statutes or by new constitutions, even if the charter or the laws contain provisions contradicting the text of the treaty.[11]

LEY (Law). The exercise of legislative power is entrusted to the National Assembly or to the National Council.[12] The former has very restricted legislative powers, while the latter has broader responsibilities, including the enactment of all laws necessary for the fulfillment of the objectives of the state.[13]

Laws enacted by the Assembly may be submitted by their special committees or by the National Legislative Council. Approval of a bill submitted to the Assembly requires a favorable vote of the majority of the members of this body. Once approved by the Assembly, the bill must be promulgated within six days from the date of enactment unless otherwise stated by the statute itself.[14] The instrument is signed by the president and the secretary of the Assembly following the statement in the text, "the National Assembly of Representatives of the *Corregimientos* of Panama decrees."[15] The assembly may not delegate any of its functions.[16]

Laws enacted by the Council may be submitted by its own members or by the Provincial Coordinating Councils through the president of the National Assembly. However, the Assembly may submit drafts before the Council through the president of the Assembly itself provided these drafts are approved by a majority vote of the originating body. The Council is then obligated to consider the bill in due course.[17]

Approval of bills is subject to procedural requirements. They must be approved in a single debating session by a majority vote of the Council. All interest groups affected by the bill submitted must be heard, as well as the affected Provincial Coordinating Councils.[18]

The instruments thus enacted are published in the official gazette within six days, after which they become enforceable unless otherwise stated in the instrument itself.[19] The published text closes with the signatures of the members of the Council.[20] Laws enacted by either body are subordinate to the constitution.[21]

DECRETO (Decree). The functions assigned to the Panamanian executive power are entrusted to a president and a vice-president of the republic. They are supported by the cabinet ministers who must countersign all the executive issuances for legal validity.[22] Under certain circumstances, the support of the National Legislative Council is prescribed for executive legislative issuances.[23] The cabinet ministers provide the required support individually or as a body called the Cabinet Council.[24]

The most important legislative function of the president is to issue regulations for the implementation of certain laws. These regulations must strictly conform to their legislative source.[25] The official gazettes indicate that regulations are passed by means of a decree. They are ordinarily signed by the president of the republic and the corresponding minister of the cabinet.

Occasionally, executive issuances are entitled executive decrees. Nevertheless, no appreciable differences were found between a decree and an executive decree. This may suggest that both are being used interchangeably.

Concerning their rank, decrees are subordinate to laws and must therefore conform to them; compliance is entrusted to the Supreme Court which may annul decrees issued in violation of the constitution and the laws. The comptroller general is responsible for compliance when decrees concern public funds or property.[26]

Publication of these instruments is required in the official gazette.

RESOLUCIÓN (Resolution). This instrument is also an executive issuance which may bear such headings as *resolución de gabinete* (cabinet resolution), *resolución ejecutiva* (executive resolution), and *resolución ministerial* (ministerial resolution). They are all subordinate to the laws and the constitution.

Cabinet resolutions originate within the Cabinet Council, an executive body consisting of the cabinet ministers and the vice-president, which is headed by the president of the republic.[27] Some of the functions entrusted to the Cabinet Council are performed by means of these issuances. In this regard, some of the Council's responsibilities are to approve the appointment of the justices of the Supreme Court by the president of the republic, to approve or reject government loans and the transfer of state property, and to support or oppose presidential decisions concerning suspension of constitutional guarantees.[28]

Executive resolutions are issued by the president of the republic with the support of one or more of the corresponding individual ministers of the cabinet. The content of executive resolutions found in several issues of the official gazette revealed that these instruments are used to control administrative matters.

Ministerial resolutions are issued by individual ministers of the cabinet upon instructions from either the president or the vice-president of the republic.[29]

Instruments bearing the simple heading Resolution have also been published in the official gazette. These instruments appear to be no different from executive resolutions in both content and format.

No reference was found in the Panamanian legal literature available concerning the authority relationship between these resolutions and the decrees described in the preceding section. The pertinent constitutional passage suggests, however, that the president may invalidate a resolution at his own discretion when it violates either a law or the constitution.[30]

The publication requirement is complied with by its insertion in the official gazette.

Notes

1. *Constitución política de la República de Panama* [of October 11, 1972], *Gaceta Oficial* (*G.O.*) (October 24, 1972); for an English version, see *Constitution of Panama, 1972* (Washington, D.C.: Organization of American States, 1974), art. 188 (hereafter cited as *Const.*).
2. Ibid., art. 272.
3. Ibid., art. 140.
4. *Reglamento interno de la Asamblea Nacional de Corregimientos* [Law no. 1 of October 19, 1973], *G.O.* (January 14, 1974) (hereafter cited as *Regl. int.*, Law 1/73); amended by Law no. 1 of October 23, 1974, *G.O.* (November 6, 1974); and by Law no. 27 of November 7, 1975, art. 261, *G.O.* (December 15, 1975).
5. *Const.*, art. 145.
6. Ibid., art. 163, no. 4.
7. *Regl. int.*, Law 1/73, art. 118.
8. *Const.*, art. 141, no. 1.
9. Ibid., art. 277.
10. Ibid., art. 274.
11. C. A. Quinteros, *Derecho constitucional* (San José, Costa Rica: Librería Litografía e Imprenta Antonio Lehmann, 1967), 1:529.
12. *Const.*, art. 129.
13. Ibid., art. 148.
14. Ibid., art. 145.
15. *Regl. int.*, Law 1/73, arts. 11 and 114.
16. *Const.*, art. 144, no. 4.
17. *Regl. int.*, Law 1/73, arts. 115A, 115B, and 115D.
18. *Const.*, art. 151.
19. *Regl. int.*, Law 1/73, art. 12.
20. Ibid., art. 8.
21. *Const.*, art. 188.
22. Ibid., arts. 155 and 167.
23. Ibid., art. 164.
24. Ibid., arts. 179 and 180.
25. Ibid., art. 164, no. 5.
26. Ibid., art. 240, nos. 2 and 7.
27. Ibid., art. 179.
28. Ibid., art. 180.
29. Ibid., art. 167.
30. Ibid.

Paraguay

1. Constitution
2. Treaties
3. Law Decree Law
4. Decree

paraguay

CONSTITUCIÓN (Constitution). The charter expressly states that the constitution is the supreme law of the nation, and that any law, decree, regulation, or act of authority contrary to it shall be null and void. It further states that the Supreme Court may declare unconstitutional any legislative instrument or part thereof which is issued in violation of this supremacy.[1] Nevertheless, only the specific case brought before the court is subject to its declaration; the court's decision does not have the effect of annulling the statute itself.[2]

Another specific provision prescribes that the charter may not be totally amended until ten years after the date of its promulgation; partial amendments are allowed after five years.[3] The decision to declare the need for a constitutional amendment must be made by the National Assembly which consists of the membership of the Chamber of Deputies, the Senate, and the Council of State. Amending the charter requires a two-thirds vote of the entire assembly membership and need not be supported by the executive branch.[4] Nevertheless, requests for the assembly to consider the need for consititutional amendment may be submitted by the executive or by either one of the congressional bodies, the Chamber or the Senate.[5]

Once the decision has been issued, a national constituent convention must be elected and established.[6] This constituent body shall only consider those parts of the constitution which the National Assembly has decided to amend except when a total reform is under consideration.[7] Partial amendments or total constitutional reforms are required to be published in the official gazette after approval by the national constituent convention.[8]

The constitution currently in force in Paraguay was sanctioned by a national constituent convention on August 25, 1967, and promulgated on that same date by the president of the republic.

TRATADO INTERNACIONAL, CONVENCIÓN INTERNACIONAL (International Treaty, International Agreement). Treaties, agreements, concordats, and other international instruments are negotiated by the president of the republic and, when completed, submitted to the legislature for final approval.[9] Congressional approval of these instruments is issued by means of an ordinary law and subject to the corresponding procedural norms.

According to the Paraguayan charter, treaties, agreements, and other international instruments in this category which are ratified and exchanged are directly subordinate to the constitution. They are above the ordinary laws and regulations.[10]

LEY (Law). This is an instrument whose issuance is entrusted to the legislature. The charter has specifically designated the Paraguayan Congress to enact, amend, and repeal codes and other laws within the framework of the constitution.[11] The charter places laws in a subordinate position to itself and international treaties and agreements.[12]

Bills may be submitted by any member of either the Chamber of Deputies or the Senate or by the president of the republic.[13] The bill containing the national budget, however, is entrusted exclusively to the president.[14] Bills related to taxation, the monetary and banking systems, the contracting of loans, the national budget, and electoral or municipal matters may only be introduced before the Chamber of Deputies. Bills concerning national defense, ratification of international treaties and agreements, and expropriation and other limitations to the right of ownership on real estate shall only be introduced to Congress through the Chamber or Senate.[15]

Bills must be considered and voted upon by both chambers of Congress. Approval is accomplished by a simple majority vote, provided that a quorum has been established.[16] The charter provides for a system of automatic approval in cases when either chamber of the legislature does not proceed on the bill or when the executive does not promulgate the enactment within the prescribed time. In the first instance, approval of the bill by the reluctant chamber is legally established, and in the second case, the enactment is considered promulgated into a law. Additional procedural norms concerning disagreements between the congressional chambers on bills have been established by the charter.[17]

Bills approved by both chambers of the legislature are forwarded to the president of the republic for either promulgation, partial objection, or total rejection. Any of these actions must take place within ten days.[18] Executive failure to do so, as indicated above, results in automatic promulgation. Partial vetoes are reconsidered by both congressional chambers which can uphold their original standing by a majority vote of their membership. Bills totally rejected by the executive require a favorable two-thirds vote of both chambers to override the veto.[19]

Laws are promulgated by the president of the republic.[20] They are enforceable only after promulgation and publication in the official register.[21] The official printed version of the laws, as found in the register, is headed with the following statement, "The congress of the Paraguayan nation sanctions with the force of law . . . ." At the conclusion of the text appears, "Be it enacted as a law of the Republic, published and entered into the Official Register."[22]

DECRETO LEY (Decree Law). The charter entrusts the executive branch with the power to enact decrees with force of law when Congress is in recess or when, for whatever reason, Congress has been dissolved. For such enactments, the executive is required to hear the opinion of the Council of State and to submit the resulting legislative instruments for the approval of the legislature within the first sixty days of the following regular congressional term.[23] Notwithstanding, decree laws take effect within the prescribed terms immediately after their publication. Subsequent congressional approval is a formality which does not interfere with their enforcement except when Congress disapproves. The latter situation poses a number of serious questions as to the retroactive effects of congressional opposition. These questions remain unanswered since there is a lack of literature on the topic. These instruments are designated decree laws and appear in the official register under that heading, followed by a serial number.

As to the rank of decree laws, the constitution seems to indicate that they share authority with the ordinary laws generated by Congress since they are issued to cover the same matters and in lieu of them.

DECRETO (Decree). The executive power is vested in the president of the republic.[24] A perusal of the national official gazette and the official register revealed that, in addition to his participation in the legislative process, the president is empowered to issue decrees under his signature to discharge all executive responsibilities. Executive decrees are also countersigned by the corresponding cabinet minister.[25] The variety of executive functions determines the variety of content for these decrees. One may find decrees appointing a low-level public official, containing regulations for the implementation of a substantive law, or declaring a state of siege which suspends some constitutional guarantees or dissolves Congress.

No legal literature was available on the Constitution of 1967 which could shed some light on whether there are any relevant ranking differences between a purely administrative decree and one bearing substantive legal provisions implementing an ordinary law.

The general context of the charter and reported practices indicate that all executive issuances must not only conform to the constitution but to the international treaties, laws, and decree laws as well.[26]

Notes

1. *Constitución de la República del Paraguay,* Official ed. (Asunción: Imprenta Nacional, 1967), arts. 8 and 11; for an English version, see *Constitution of the Republic of Paraguay, 1967* (Washington, D.C.: Organization of American States, 1969).
2. Ibid., art. 200.
3. Ibid., art. 219.
4. Ibid., art. 220.
5. Ibid., art. 221.
6. Ibid., arts. 222 to 225.
7. Ibid., art. 226.
8. Ibid., art. 231.
9. Ibid., arts, 180, no. 6; and 149, no. 8.
10. Ibid., art. 8.
11. Ibid., art. 149, no. 1.
12. Ibid., art. 8.
13. Ibid., art. 154.
14. Ibid., art. 163.
15. Ibid., arts. 151, no. 1; and 153, nos. 1 and 2.
16. Ibid., arts. 147 and 155.
17. Ibid., arts. 155, 160, 161, and 162.
18. Ibid., art. 155.
19. Ibid., arts. 157 and 158.
20. Ibid., arts. 155 to 158; 162; and 180, no. 3.
21. Ibid., art. 165.

22. Ibid., art. 166.
23. Ibid., arts. 183; and 190, no. 1.
24. Ibid., art. 171.
25. Ibid., art. 184.
26. Ibid., arts. 176; and 180, nos. 3, 5, 11, and 12.

PERU

Under the Constitution

1. Constitution
2. Treaties   Law
3. Supreme Decree
4. Supreme Resolution

Current Status

1. Constitution   Decree Law
2. Treaties
3. Supreme Decree
4. Supreme Resolution

CONSTITUCIÓN (Constitution). Even though the charter is not expressly acknowledged as the fundamental law of the land, its supremacy is clearly established by the fact that control of conformity thereto has been entrusted to high-ranking state bodies.[1] In addition, the charter provides for a special procedure to be observed when amendments are to be executed. In this regard, any constitutional amendment must be approved by both houses of the legislature, the Chamber of Deputies and the so-called Functional Senate. Approval by both chambers requires an additional ratification by both legislative bodies. Approval and ratification take place when such actions are supported by an absolute majority of the membership of each chamber. Members of the legislature or the president of the republic may propose amendments. In the latter case, support of the Council of Ministers of the cabinet is required.[2] All aspects of the charter may be amended except for the provisions concerning the reelection of the president of the republic for the following term.[3]

Constitutional amendments are enacted in the form of an ordinary law with a corresponding serial number and published in the official national gazette, or in any other national newspaper, if so indicated.[4]

The constitution currently in force in Peru was sanctioned by a constituent Congress on March 29, 1933, and promulgated by the president of the republic on April 9, 1933. It has been amended a number of times.

Current Status. A military coup overthrew the constitutional president in the early days of October 1968. Even though the new de facto government claimed it would adhere to the constitution to the extent it was compatible with the objectives of the "revolutionary government," a decree law was issued establishing the new legal foundations upon which the regime would erect its political structure.[5] The new statute did not expressly provide for the assignment of constituent power. Nevertheless, the fact that the government offically declared it would abide by the constitution only insofar as it did not interfere with the stated objectives of the revolution indicates that the government does exercise the power to amend the charter as it sees fit. The exercise of this power was demonstrated by the executive issuance of legislative instruments in direct opposition to the charter and by their consequent enforcement by the courts.

The latest available official edition of the charter includes two decree laws issued by the military junta containing provisions broadening the scope of some constitutional provisions.[6] These instruments were issued by the president of the republic with the approval of the Council of Ministers of the cabinet acting jointly with the military junta and pursuant to the provisions of the so-called Statute of the Revolutionary Government.[7]

As far as it has been possible to ascertain, there is no definitive version of the Peruvian charter which incorporates all the amendatory provisions issued by the military government. Only partially updated texts have been published through September 1977.

LEY (Law). This is a legislative instrument generated by the legislature pursuant to the constitutional provisions granting this body the power to enact, interpret, amend, and repeal the laws of the republic.[8] As indicated above, the Peruvian legislature is a bicameral organization consisting of the Functional Senate and the Chamber of Deputies.[9] The designated Senate was never appointed, and an elected Senate was established instead.[10] In addition to the law, the legislature issues an instrument to cover other matters designated *resolución legislativa* (legislative resolution).[11]

Bills for statutory enactments and proposals for legislative resolutions may be submitted by members of the Chamber of Deputies, the Senate, the Supreme Court (on matters concerning the judiciary), and the executive branch.[12] Bills relating to personal rewards resulting in disbursement by the national treasury, salary increases for civil servants, and the national budget are entrusted to the exclusive initiative of the executive branch.[13]

Bills are debated and voted upon in both the Chamber and the Senate. Impasses and differences are settled by a joint session of both bodies in Congress.[14]

Legislative instruments that have been approved by Congress are sent to the executive power. The pertinent constitutional passages are not altogether clear in this respect. Nevertheless, according to practices reported by a Peruvian author, the president does exercise veto power against approved congressional instruments submitted to it for promulgation.[15]

Laws must be promulgated by the president of the republic within ten days. If he fails to do so, Congress does by ordering their publication in the designated newspaper.[16] The text of the law is ordinarily introduced by the statement, "The Congress of the Peruvian Republic has enacted the following law" and is concluded by, "Let it be communicated to the Executive Power for Promulgation." The promulgation itself begins with, "The President of the Republic: Whereas Congress has enacted the following law" and ends with, "Therefore, I order that it be published and observed."[17]

Laws are enforceable from the day after their publication, except when the law itself provides otherwise.[18]

No constitutional provision has been found assigning a specific rank to the laws. Nevertheless, the Peruvian Civil Code provides that in cases of conflict between the constitution and a law the former shall prevail, thus clearly reaffirming constitutional supremacy.[19]

Current Status. The Statute of the Revolutionary Government provides that the legislative functions entrusted to Congress under the charter are now assigned to the president of the republic who shall exercise them with the support of the Council of Ministers of the cabinet and the revolutionary junta. The resulting legislative instruments are designated decree laws.[20]

A number of issues of the newspaper *El Peruano* revealed that decree laws may be identified under the direct heading *decreto ley* followed by the corresponding serial number. The instrument is signed by the president of the republic, all cabinet ministers, and the members of the revolutionary junta.

Since decree laws have replaced ordinary laws as provided by the charter, the former instruments not only share rank with the latter but also may be above the constitution. They can bear provisions which, in some instances, prevail over the constitution and amend it.

TRATADO INTERNACIONAL (International Treaty). There is no legal provision in either the charter or any other available source assigning a hierarchy to international treaties and agreements within the Peruvian legislative system. Only general guidelines were found in the legal literature concerning some aspects of the process by which international agreements are approved and enacted into law.[21] The basic constitutional provisions concerning this topic prescribed that international treaties and agreements are negotiated by the president of the republic with the approval of the Council of Ministers. The completed instrument is then submitted to Congress for its approval.[22] Examination of the official newspaper indicated that some international instruments are both negotiated and approved only by the executive branch by means of an instrument called the supreme resolution (*resolución suprema*), although there are no specific provisions assigning the responsibility of approving international instruments to the executive. Nevertheless, Peruvian authors reported that established official practices have determined that international agreements relating to matters falling within the competence of the executive branch need only be covered by executive approval. Those concerning matters within the competence of Congress are subject to its approval.[23]

Current Status. Perusing the official newspaper revealed that international instruments are approved by decree laws at present. These executive issuances may or may not contain the text of the international instrument. It has also been observed that the supreme resolution, another executive instrument, is being used, in limited instances, for the approval of international treaties and agreements. No reasons were given in any of the sources for this differentiation between the two channels of approval. Further examination of the official newspaper also revealed that texts of international instruments may be published by themselves, separated from the approving legislative instrument. The charter of the revolutionary government does not refer to international instruments except to state that the Peruvian government honors and respects the international treaties and agreements entered into by the republic.[24]

DECRETO SUPREMO (Supreme Decree). The Peruvian charter empowers the president of the republic to issue regulations for the implementation of the laws which may not oppose or misinterpret the laws. The same restrictions are extended to decrees and resolutions issued by the executive branch with the same purpose.[25] The official newspaper and a national scholar indicate that, in practice, the Peruvian executive issues supreme decrees and supreme resolutions to carry out his regulatory responsibilities.[26]

No statutory standards have been found which determine the matters specifically assigned to supreme decrees. According to the scholar consulted, supreme decrees are issued to cover substantive matters and implement the general provisions of a statute. However, an analysis of legislative material published in the official newspaper indicates that the proposed criteria have not always been followed. For instance, there are ministerial resolutions implementing substantive statutes, instruments of lower rank than supreme decrees.

Supreme decrees are immediately subordinate to the national charter and the laws enacted to carry out its objectives. These instruments are, according to the opinion of one author, the highest ranking instrument of executive issuance.[27] There are no statutory provisions concerning this latter statement in the available sources.

Supreme decrees are issued under the signature of the president of the republic and the corresponding minister or ministers of the cabinet.[28] A Peruvian source reports that decree laws are submitted to the Council of Ministers of the cabinet for discussion and approval before they are signed.[29] But there is no statutory evidence supporting this assertion. Publication of these instruments is ordinarily made in the official newspaper.

Current Status. No changes have taken place concerning legislative instruments of executive issuance as established by the present charter.

RESOLUCIÓN SUPREMA (Supreme Resolution). In addition to supreme decrees, the president of the republic may also issue supreme resolutions to implement the ordinary statutes of congressional origin. There are no specific provisions in either the charter or its implementing statutes concerning the matters to be assigned to each of these executive instruments. Examination of both indicates that there are no substantive differences between the two except for their format. Supreme resolutions do not bear the full signature of the president of the republic but only his initials or *rúbrica* and the countersignature of the corresponding minister of the cabinet.

Concerning the hierarchical rank of supreme resolutions, a Peruvian scholar stated that supreme resolutions are assigned a rank subordinate to the supreme decrees and hence to the laws and the constitution.[30]

The reader of Peruvian legal sources should also know that there are other kinds of resolutions in the Peruvian system issued at various cabinet levels. These ministerial resolutions may or may not cover matters which ordinarily are assigned to supreme resolutions. A legal source suggests that this apparent delegation of presidential prerogatives takes place when the chief executive cannot find the time to perform these functions directly or when to demand direct presidential action.[31] A perusal of the official newspaper reveals that ministerial resolutions may even carry regulatory material. The hierarchical rank of supreme resolutions is not refered to in the statutes. Nevertheless, it has been suggested that they rank below the supreme decrees.[32] They are printed in the official newspaper.

Current Status. This legislative instrument of executive issuance has not changed under the current circumstances.

Notes

1. F. Bonilla, *Constitución Política del Perú*, 11th ed. (Lima: Editorial Mercurio S.A., 1974), arts 26, p. 13; 123, no. 4, p. 28; and 133, p. 32 (hereafter cited as Bonilla, *Const.*).
2. Ibid., art. 236, p. 52.
3. Ibid., art. 142, pp. 33 and 34.
4. Ibid., art. 129, p. 31.
5. *Estatuto del gobierno revolucionario de la fuerza armada*, Decree law 17,063 of October 3, 1968, in Bonilla, *Const.*, art. 5, p. 100 (hereafter cited as *Estatuto*).
6. Ibid.
7. Ibid., art. 6, pp. 100 and 101.
8. Bonilla, *Const.*, art. 123, no. 1, p. 28.
9. Ibid., art. 89, p. 22.
10. J. Pareja Paz-Soldán, *Derecho constitutional peruano*, 5th ed. (Lima: Ediciones Librería Studium, 1973), pp. 286 and 287 (hereafter cited as Pareja, *Derecho*).
11. Bonilla, *Const.*, art. 154, no. 6, p. 36.
12. Ibid., art. 124, p. 30.
13. Ibid., arts. 120, p. 28; and 177, p. 40.
14. Ibid., arts. 125 to 127, pp. 30 and 31.
15. Ibid., arts. 129, p. 31; and 6 (transitory), p. 53; Pareja, *Derecho*, pp. 248 to 252; J. Pareja Paz-Soldán, *Las constituciones del Perú* (Madrid: Ediciones Cultura Hispánica, 1954), pp. 345 to 351.
16. Bonilla, *Const.*, arts. 128 and 129, p. 31.
17. Ibid., art. 130, p. 31.
18. Ibid., art. 132, p. 31.
19. *Código Civil*, 1st ed. (Lima: Editorial Juris S.A., 1975), art. XXII, titulo preliminar.
20. *Estatuto* in Bonilla, *Const.*, art. 6, pp. 100 and 101.
21. Pareja, *Derecho*, p. 246.
22. Bonilla, *Const.*, arts. 123, no. 21, p. 30; and 154, no. 20, p. 37.
23. Pareja, *Derecho*, p. 246.
24. *Estatuto* in Bonilla, *Const.*, art. 7, p. 101.
25. Bonilla, *Const.*, art. 154, no. 8, p. 36.
26. Pareja, *Derecho*, p. 248.
27. D. B. Furnish, "The Hierarchy of Peruvian Laws: Context for Law and Development," *American Journal of Comparative Law* 19 (1971): 113 (hereafter cited as Furnish, "Hierarchy").
28. Bonilla, *Const.*, art. 166, p. 39.
29. Furnish, "Hierarchy," p. 113.
30. Ibid., p. 115; *Bonilla, Const.*, arts. 133, p. 32; and 154, no. 8, p. 36.
31. F. Tola, *Derecho administrativo del Perú*, part 1 (Lima: Universidad Nacional Mayor de San Marcos, 1945), p. 81.
32. Furnish, "Hierarchy," p. 115.

salvador

1. Constitution

2. [Legislative] Accord [Legislative] Decree Treaties

3. (Executive) Decree (Executive) Accord

SALVADOR

CONSTITUCIÓN (Constitution). Under the terms of the Salvadorean charter currently in force, the constitution is paramount in the nation's legislative system. According to its pertinent passages, the charter prevails over all laws, regulations, decrees, orders, and resolutions issued by the executive branch.[1] Legislative instruments violating this norm are annulled and stripped of any legal effect. Laws, decrees, and regulations opposing the charter may formally be declared unconstitutional by the Supreme Court.[2] Furthermore, any court of law may decide in the specific cases submitted to their jurisdiction on the inapplicability of executive legislative issuances deemed contrary to the constitution. These decisions are only binding for the parties concerned.[3]

Constitutional predominance is further reaffirmed in the charter's amendment procedures. Bills with constitutionally amendatory content may be introduced by a two-thirds vote of the elected representatives of the Legislative Assembly. The resolution adopted must specifically refer to the constitutional provisions to be affected by the proposed amendments and contain the text of the amended version to be considered. This information is then published in the official gazette. The bill is placed on the agenda of the next term of the Legislative Assembly. If this assembly ratifies the bill, a constituent assembly is then convened to decide whether the amendments proposed are to be enacted.[4]

No provisions were found in the charter concerning the instrument through which constitutional amendments are enacted. Examination of the national official gazette did not reveal any amendments to the current charter, which was enacted on January 8, 1962, and took effect eight days after its publication in the national official gazette.[5]

DECRETO [LEGISLATIVO] ([Legislative] Decree). The legislative power is vested in a Legislative Assembly which under the terms of the charter may not delegate its prerogatives to the other branches of the government.[6] Basic functions of the Legislative Assembly are the enactment, interpretation, amendment, and repeal of laws.[7] The constitution includes a number of provisions controlling the law enactment process.[8] A perusal of the official gazette indicates that in El Salvador the Legislative Assembly exercises its powers by means of legislative decrees, which are not referred to in the constitution. Nevertheless, a large number of legislative decrees are published covering legal matters, and no differences have been observed between the content of legislative decrees and laws as prescribed by the charter. These facts suggest that legislative decrees are probably the instruments of promulgation whose provisions constitute the laws of the nation as issued by the legislature.

Bills for the enactment of legislative decrees may be introduced by the deputies of the Legislative Assembly, the president of the republic through the ministers of his cabinet, and the Supreme Court of Justice.[9] Bills introducing provisions interpreting, amending, or repealing any part of the codes of the nation that are not introduced by the Supreme Court require that the opinion of this high tribunal be heard before the legislature may initiate its debates upon these proposed bills.[10] A majority vote is sufficient for the assembly to make a valid decision provided that no less than two-thirds of the membership is attending the session. If attendance does not reach that proportion, a two-thirds vote of the attending members cast in support of the decision shall be required.[11]

After approval, bills are sent to the executive branch for sanctioning before promulgation or vetoing. The latter requires that executive action be taken within eight days. For some cases specifically prescribed by the constitution, legislative decrees do not require executive sanctioning.[12] Bills affected by executive veto are sent back to the assembly for debating and voting. A two-thirds vote of the entire assembly's membership is required to reaffirm the original standing of the bill, in which case the executive is compelled to sanction it.[13] When the executive veto is founded on grounds of unconstitutionality but the assembly still insists on reaffirmation, the Supreme Court participates in the process by deciding whether or not the enactment is legally viable.[14]

Under the Salvadorean charter, legislative enactments take effect eight days after their date of promulgation and publication by the executive.[15] When promulgation and publication are not performed by the executive branch the Legislative Assembly does so and the resulting enactment becomes enforceable within ten days. These instruments may be published in either the official newspaper or in the newspaper with the widest national circulation.[16]

The constitution has specifically assigned legislative decrees and related regulatory statutes to a rank immediately below itself.

ACUERDO [LEGISLATIVO] ([Legislative] Accord). Examination of the Salvadorean official gazette reveals that the Legislative Assembly also issues accords as part of its legislative responsibilities. There are no provisions in the charter which either directly or indirectly refer to this category of legislative issuances. This situation and the additional problem of an absolute lack of literature on the topic make it impossible to attempt a description of the differences that may exist between accords and legislative decrees.

The accords found covered such matters as taxation and acceptance of foreign decorations by private citizens.

No specific provisions were found in the constitution or elsewhere concerning the hierarchical rank of accords, except the general principle concerning constitutional predominance over all forms of legislative issuances.[17]

TRATADO INTERNACIONAL (International Treaty). International treaties, agreements, and related instruments are negotiated and approved by the president of the republic.[18] After executive approval they must be submitted to the Legislative Assembly for ratification.[19] Approval and ratification are achieved by means of an executive instrument designated the *acuerdo* (accord) and by the legislative decree, respectively.

Enactment apparently still requires the issuance of an instrument of ratification by the president of the republic which is then published in the official gazette.

Neither the charter nor its regulatory legislation referred to the rank asssigned to international treaties and agreements. Finally, the absolute unavailability of legal literature on the topic prevented the authors of this study from formulating any opinion as to the level of authority of these international instruments in El Salvador.

DECRETO (Decree). The performance of executive functions is entrusted to the president of the republic, his ministers of the cabinet, and the undersecretaries of state. The president issues decrees, accords, *órdenes* (orders), and *providencias* (instructions). Each of these instruments must be "authorized and communicated," the latter presumably to the people, by the ministers of the cabinet of the respective department. The absence of this formality renders the instrument unenforceable.[20] There are no specific provisions in the charter or elsewhere assigning the above instruments to any particular matters or areas of executive concern.

Examination of the official gazette suggests that decrees may be the most relevant of all the executive instruments since they ordinarily include the regulatory provisions issued by the executive in pursuance of a given legislative decree.[21] In some instances decrees are also issued to establish and organize governmental agencies.

When the legislature is in recess, the executive branch may exercise extraordinary powers affecting constitutional guarantees. It may issue a decree suspending those guarantees, in which case the president is required to act with the consent of the Council of Ministers of the cabinet. The Legislative Assembly is automatically convened to approve or reject the decree concerned within forty-eight hours.[22]

Ordinarily, executive decrees take effect twelve days after the date of their insertion in the official gazette.[23]

Pursuant to the charter and the civil code, decrees are subordinate to the laws, that is, legislative decrees, and ultimately to the constitution.[24]

ACUERDO (Accord). Referred to in the previous section, the accord is another instrument of executive issuance. There are no apparent differences between decrees and accords vis-à-vis format and content. A difficulty in assessing this instrument is the unavailability of literature on this topic. A considerable number of issues of the official gazette examined reveal that, by and large, accords cover matters not necessarily of general interest, such as granting legal status to juristic persons and authorizing payment to certain private individuals. The more significant and likely content of an accord was found to be executive approval of an international treaty and submission thereof to the Legislative Assembly for ratification.

No provisions were found in the charter or in any other related sources which concerned the authority rank of executive accords. One must assume there is a general principle that all laws, regulations, etc., are subordinate to the constitution.[25] Written sources have not been able to establish differences between the two executive issuances: decrees and accords.

Notes

1. *Constitución Política de la República de El Salvador, 1962* (San Salvador: Presidencia de la República, 1975), arts. 80 and 220; for an English version, see *Constitution of the Republic of El Salvador, 1962* (Washington, D.C.: Organization of American States, 1966) (hereafter cited as *Const.*).
2. Ibid., art. 96.
3. Ibid., art. 95.
4. Ibid., art. 222.
5. Ibid., art. 228.
6. Ibid., arts. 4 and 36.
7. Ibid., art. 47, no. 12.
8. Ibid., arts. 50 to 61.
9. Ibid., art. 50.
10. Ibid., art. 61.
11. Ibid., art. 39.
12. Ibid., arts. 51 and 52.
13. Ibid., art. 52.
14. Ibid., art. 53.
15. Ibid., arts. 51 to 53 and 60.
16. Ibid., art. 54.
17. Ibid., art. 220.
18. Ibid., art. 78, no. 12.
19. Ibid., art. 147, no. 29.
20. Ibid., art. 75.
21. Ibid., art. 78, no. 15.
22. Ibid., art. 176.
23. *Código Civil* (Madrid: Instituto de Cúltura Hispánica, 1959), arts. 6 and 7.
24. *Const.*, arts. 80 and 129.
25. Ibid.

URUGUAY

Under the Constitution

1. Constitution

2. Law Treaties

3. Decree

Current Status

1. Constitution Institutional Act (or Decree)

2. Law Treaties

3. Decree

CONSTITUCIÓN (Constitution). The Uruguayan charter was enacted by its General Assembly on August 24, 1966. It was also approved by a plebiscite on September 27, 1966, to take effect on February 15, 1967.[1]

The supreme authority of the constitution stems not from a direct and express mandate of the charter itself but from a number of its provisions which establish special procedural norms for the adjudication of cases affected by the constitution and related statutes.[2] These cases are entrusted to the highest court of the nation, the Supreme Court, whose decision only affects the parties concerned and does not render a given statute unconstitutional for all.[3] The court declares the statute or regulation inapplicable to each case exclusively.

Consistent with the principle of constitutional precedence, the charter provides its own special amendatory procedure. Constitutional amendments may be either total or partial and may be conducted in two different ways.[4] The first set of rules involves a number of steps to be followed depending on the amendment's initiator. The initiative can come from either 10 percent of the citizenry, the General Assembly, the senators, the representatives of the legislative chamber, or the executive power consisting of the president of the republic with the support of one or more of his cabinet ministers. The amendatory drafts must be filed with the General Assembly for approval and subsequent promulgation by the president of the assembly. Thereafter, the executive shall convene a national constituent convention which decides on the viability of the draft by an absolute majority vote. The approved amendatory draft is then forwarded to the executive for its publication and for submission to the electorate for scrutiny and a decision. The plebiscite decides on the amendment by a simple majority vote which must represent at least 35 percent of the total number of registered voters.[5]

The second procedure provides for constitutional amendments by means of the constitutional statute or law (*ley constitutional*), the passage of which requires a two-thirds vote of both the Chamber of Representatives and the Senate. No presidential veto is allowed in this case; the constitutional law must also be submitted to the electorate for approval. The constitutional statute is promulgated by the president of the General Assembly.[6]

Current Status. The president of the republic dissolved both the Chamber of Representatives and the Senate by a Decree of June 27, 1973.[7] With the same instrument, he created the *Consejo de Estado* (Council of State), allegedly to replace the legislature, to control executive actions, and to draft a new constitution.

The armed forces issued a communiqué to the people on June 12, 1976, informing them of the withdrawal of their support from the president and of their decision to substitute constitutional statutes for the new constitution proposed by the president to govern the transitional period.[8]

A Constitutional Decree of June 12, 1976, suspended an election that was imminent.[9] This action was immediately followed by another decree of the same date, creating the *Consejo de la Nación* (Council of the Nation) which assumed the functions previously entrusted to the Council of State. One of these functions was the drafting of a new charter following guidelines which were to be drawn up. The second decree also entrusted the Council of Ministers of the cabinet, acting jointly with the National Security Council, with the responsibility of defining national objectives and formulating guidelines for action. Finally, the decree repealed all constitutional provisions which, directly or indirectly, opposed the provisions set forth therein.[10]

Five more decrees containing the so-called *actas institucionales* (institutional acts) were issued as of April 1977. They may be identified by the signatures of the president of the republic and two ministers of the cabinet pursuant to the provisions of Decree 14/977.[11] They were published in the official gazette, *Diario Oficial.*

LEY (Law). Under the charter, the legislative power is entrusted to the General Assembly which consists of the Chamber of Representatives and the Senate.[12] As such, this body has been granted the power to enact codes and laws.[13]

Bills may be originated by or submitted before either the Chamber of Representatives or the Senate, by their respective members or the executive branch through the ministers of the cabinet.[14] Bills concerning the national public debt and public credit, establishment of public offices, increases in salaries and retirement pensions, or any other money compensation may only be submitted by the executive branch.[15]

Bills must be debated in both the Chamber of Representatives and the Senate. Disagreements between the two legislative bodies are resolved in joint sessions by a two-thirds vote.[16] Bills approved by both legislative bodies are forwarded to the executive branch for either approval and promulgation or veto within ten days.[17] If vetoed, the affected bill is reconsidered by a joint session of the legislature, which is the General Assembly. The assembly's decisions must be supported by a three-fifths vote of the attending membership. Failure on the part of the assembly to issue a decision within sixty days is technically interpreted as legislative concurrence with the executive objections.[18] Objections formulated by the executive branch and the required legislative process to follow must be published in the official gazette.[19] Executive approval of legislative bills and subsequent promulgation are performed by the president of the republic[20] in this form: "The Senate and the Chamber of Representatives of the Oriental Republic of Uruguay, convened in General Assembly, decree: . . . ."[21] The instrument is signed by the president of the republic and the appropriate minister or ministers of his cabinet.[22] Laws thus enacted are published by order of the president in the official gazette.[23]

They are enforceable ten days after the date of promulgation in the capital. It is apparent that under the provisions of the Uruguayan Civil Code, promulgation and publication are synonymous and take place simultaneously.[24]

Regarding the authority rank of the law, it is generally understood that this category of legislative instrument is immediately subordinate to the constitution.

Current Status. As stated above, both the Chamber of Representatives and the Senate were dissolved by an executive decree in 1973.[25] The Council of State was established instead to carry out basic legislative functions of which the most important is issuing national laws. Bills concerning matters which, under the charter, were exclusively entrusted to the executive branch continue to require its approval.[26]

Under the present circumstances, the executive power, supported by the Council of National Security and the Council of Ministers, submit, bills to the Council of State on matters concerning municipalities, decentralized agencies, civic and electoral registers, protocol, and related activities.[27]

Laws issued by the Council of State bear the signatures of its president and secretaries.[28] They are then promulgated by the president and published in the official gazette.

There are no provisions concerning the hierarchical ranking of these issuances. One can only guess that within the current context, laws issued by the Council of State would have to conform to the institutional acts, the sources which define general objectives and provide guidelines to achieve these goals. In addition, institutional acts were found to contain fundamental principles aimed at building the foundation of the promised future constitution.[29]

TRATADO INTERNACIONAL (International Treaty). Under the provisions of the Uruguayan charter, international treaties and agreements are negotiated by the executive power; they must either be approved or rejected by the General Assembly; and finally, they are ratified by the executive branch.[30] Examination of the content of official gazettes indicates that the negotiating phase of a treaty ordinarily ends with the issuance of a decree by the executive approving the instrument and ordering that it be forwarded to the General Assembly. The assembly expresses approval by enacting a law to that effect. No instrument of executive issuance has been found which performs the last formality of ratification required by the charter.

A perusal of the text of a number of decrees, resolutions, and laws related to international instruments has revealed that, in some instances, international treaties and agreements have been approved directly by the president of the republic with no mention of any required action by the legislature.[31]

Current Status. Under the present state of affairs, international treaties and agreements are approved by laws enacted by means of an executive decree. There are no statutory provisions establishing this procedure; nevertheless, the content of official gazettes offers strong evidence to this effect.

There are no indications as to the hierarchical rank of international instruments in the Uruguayan legislative system either in the constitution or elsewhere. Monographic contributions on the topic are rather scarce and only of a very general nature.

DECRETO (Decree). Under the charter, executive power is exercised by the president of the republic who discharges his duties with the support and assistance of the ministers of the cabinet, individually or as a body in the Council of Ministers.[32] The council is headed by the president and is entrusted with specific functions as assigned by the constitution.[33] Among these is the power to overrule decisions made by the president of the republic, even those which are supported by one or more ministers, provided that such decision is supported by an absolute majority vote of the attending membership of the council.[34]

A basic legislative function entrusted to the president of the republic by the constitution is that of issuing the regulations necessary for implementing the laws.[35] The president performs this task by issuing a decree, a regulatory instrument which must bear the signatures of the chief executive and at least one of the ministers of the cabinet in order to be enforced.[36]

Decrees are subordinate to the laws and ultimately to the constitution.[37] Publication of these instruments in the official gazette is required.

Current Status. According to Decree 333/976, currently there is a president of the republic appointed by the Council of the Nation. The instrument provides for the president to discharge his assigned responsibilities by means of decrees with the assistance of one or more ministers of the cabinet, the Council of National Security, or the Council of Ministers of the Cabinet.[38] Special procedural provisions cover the formal aspects of the issuance when it is made with another body. For instance, when a decree is issued with the support of the Council of National Security, the instrument must be signed by the president and countersigned by the minister of the interior and of national defense.[39] The decree promulgates a law and the institutional acts must be signed by the president and the corresponding minister or ministers of the cabinet. Decrees of a general nature, that is, those not specifically mentioned by Constitutional Decree 3/976, shall bear either the initials of the president or his partial signature and the countersignature of the minister or ministers of the cabinet concerned. Acts entrusted to the exclusive responsibility of the president are signed by him alone.[40]

There are a very limited number of provisions controlling executive responsibilities and related functions.

Notes

1. *Constitución de la República Oriental del Uruguay (1967), Diario Oficial* (February 2, 1967); for an English version, see *Constitution of the Republic of Uruguay* (Washington, D.C.: Organization of American States, 1967) (hereafter cited as *Const.*).

2. Ibid., arts. 256 to 261.

3. Ibid., art. 259.

4. Ibid., art. 331.

5. Ibid., art. 331 A, B, and C.

6. Ibid., art. 331 D.

7. Decree 464/973 of June 27, 1973, *D.O.* (July 4, 1973) (hereafter cited as Decree 464/973).

8. Communiqué of the Joint Forces of June 12, 1976, *D.O.* (June 16, 1976).

9. Constitutional Decree 332/976 of June 12, 1976, Institutional Act No. 1, *D.O.* (June 28, 1976) (hereafter cited as Const. Decree 332/976).

10. Constitutional Decree 333/976 of June 12, 1976, Institutional Act No. 2, *D.O.* (June 28, 1976) (hereafter cited as Const. Decree 333/976).

11. Decree 14/977 of January 5, 1977, *D.O.* (January 13, 1977) (hereafter cited as Decree 14/977).

14. Ibid., art. 133.

15. Ibid., arts. 85, no. 6; and 86.

16. Ibid., arts. 134 and 135.

17. Ibid., arts. 135 to 137.

18. Ibid., art. 138.

19. Ibid., art. 141.

20. Ibid., arts. 143 to 145.

21. Ibid., art. 146.

22. Ibid., art. 168, no. 25.

23. Ibid., arts. 136; and 168, no. 4.

24. H. Gatti and H. J. Cerruti Aicardi, *Código Civil de la República Oriental del Uruguay, anotado* (Montevideo: Barreiro y Ramos, S.A., 1968), art. 1.

25. Decree 464/973.

26. Decree 392/976 of June 30, 1976, *D.O.* (July 8, 1976); Const. Decree 333/976.

27. Const. Decree 333/976.

28. Decree 14/977.

29. Const. Decree 333/976, art. 8.

30. *Const.*, arts, 85, no. 7; and 168, no. 20.

31. *Registro Nacional de Leyes y Decretos, 1972* (Montevideo: Imprenta Nacional, 1973), I:954 and 1,210.

32. *Const.*, art. 149.

33. Ibid., art. 160.

34. Ibid., art. 165.

35. Ibid., art. 168, no. 4.

36. Ibid., art. 168, no. 25.

37. Ibid., art. 309.

38. Constitutional Decree no. 3/976 of September 10, 1976, Institutional Act No. 3, *D.O.* (September 9, 1976).

39. Ibid.

40. Decree 14/977.

venezuela

1. Constitution

2. Law Treaties

3. Decree

venezuela

CONSTITUCIÓN (Constitution). Constitutional predominance is clearly established by the Venezuelan charter. The pertinent passage prescribes that laws issued and acts performed either by the legislative or the executive powers of the state may be declared null and void by the Supreme Court on the grounds of unconstitutionality.[1]

Under the terms of the current national constitution, originally enforced by congressional approval on January 23, 1961, and partially amended on May 9, 1973, the charter may be partially or totally amended. Partial amendments may be proposed by one-fourth of the members of either of the two chambers of Congress; or, because Venezuela is a federally organized nation, by one-fourth of the legislative assemblies of the states, provided that these proposals were supported by a majority vote of the assembly's membership in at least two separate debating sessions. In the case of proposals introduced by the chambers of the federal Congress, the members sponsoring the draft must introduce it before their own chamber. If a proposal is introduced by a state assembly, the draft is put before the Senate. The ensuing procedural steps are exactly the same as those prescribed for the passage of an ordinary national law. Once the amendatory bill has been approved by Congress, it is forwarded to every state assembly for ratification or rejection, a decision that must be made by a majority vote of the members. In an ordinary session of the following congressional term, both chambers jointly compute the ballots of the assemblies after which they declare the provisions of the amendments enacted by a two-thirds vote of the assemblies.

Partial amendments are assigned sequential numbers and published following the text of the charter. The affected articles are footnoted with references to the source and date of the amendment concerned.[2]

Total amendments may only be proposed by one-third of the members of Congress, or by an absolute majority of the state assemblies when the proposal has been favorably voted upon by an absolute majority of the members of each assembly in at least two separate debating sessions. Proposals meeting this requirement should then be presented to the office of the president of the national Congress who convenes the two legislative chambers in a joint session. Admission of the submitted proposals for congressional consideration requires a two-thirds vote of the membership attending the session. Once admitted, the proposal is debated in the chamber that Congress designates. Thereafter, the bill follows the procedural steps prescribed for ordinary laws. Once approved, the bill is submitted to a plebiscite and, if ratified by a majority vote, the legislative chambers jointly declare the new constitution approved.[3]

The president of the republic is not granted veto power over either partial or total amendments. He is therefore compelled to promulgate within ten days. Failing to do so, the president and the vice-president of Congress proceed by inserting the new text either in the national official gazette or in the congressional gazette.[4]

LEY (Law). The legislative power is vested in the Congress, consisting of two chambers, the Senate and the Chamber of Deputies.[5] According to the Venezuelan charter, legislative issuances by both chambers in their capacity as colegislators are designated laws. When these issuances include a systematic body of provisions related to one subject matter or area of concern, they are designated codes.[6] The charter provides for still another category of instrument at the same level, the organic law. Neither the constitution nor other sources provide a conceptual definition of this instrument which identifies its specific areas of concern, subject matter, and format. The authors of this study only found the following statement: "Organic laws are those so designated by this constitution as well as those to which such designation is given by decision of the absolute majority of the membership of each legislative chamber when debating upon the respective specific bill." The constitution further provides that laws enacted on matters already governed by organic laws shall conform to the latter.[7]

Except when otherwise provided for, bills for legislative enactments may be introduced before either chamber[8] by the *Comisión Delegada del Congreso* (Delegated Commission of Congress), the permanent commissions of either chamber, the executive branch, at least three senators or deputies, the citizenry when consisting of at least twenty-thousand voters, or the Supreme Court when the bills submitted are related to judicial organization or procedures.[9]

There are some exceptions to the above. For example, the bill containing the national budget is entrusted to the exclusive initiative of the executive branch and must be introduced before either legislative chamber.[10] There are also bills which must be introduced to one specific chamber. These exceptions are listed in the charter.[11]

Bills must be debated at least twice in each chamber. If the chambers cannot agree on a particular bill, they must hold a joint session to settle the matter. Bills already approved by one chamber are debated in only one session by the other if its members declare the bill urgent.[12]

Bills that have already been approved by Congress must display the heading, "The Congress of the Republic of Venezuela, Decrees: . . .,"[13] and are then forwarded to the president of the republic for either promulgation or veto. Presidential veto powers require the support of the Council of Ministers of the cabinet and must be exercised within ten days. Vetoed bills are returned to Congress for reconsideration in a joint session. Reaffirmation of the congressional standing on the bill in order to override the presidential veto requires a two-thirds vote of the membership attending the joint session. In cases where only simple majority support is obtained in Congress, the president has the choice of promulgating the law as vetoed or returning the bill to Congress within five days for final reconsideration. In this case, congressional decision is final even if supported by a simple majority. The executive then promulgates the law as issued by Congress.[14]

Vetoes formulated on the grounds of unconstitutionality entitle the president to ask the Supreme Court for a decision on the matter within the same ten days. If the Supreme Court rules against the presidential veto, the president is compelled to promulgate the law as originally issued by Congress.[15]

Promulgation of the law is performed by inserting the legislative text in the official gazette along with the president's order that it be complied with and observed. This order is in Spanish, with the word *cúmplase* closing the text.[16]

As stated previously, the president's failure to comply with the procedural requirements triggers congressional promulgation instead. In the latter case insertion of the text is made either in the official or the congressional gazette.[17]

The time when laws approving international treaties and agreements are promulgated is left to executive discretion, in accordance with international practices and the convenience of the republic.[18]

Under the Venezuelan charter, laws amending previous legislation are not promulgated separately from the amended texts, unlike the practice in some jurisdictions. The new amendatory issuance must include the entire text as amended.[19] Laws are enforceable as of the date of publication or promulgation, unless otherwise stated in the law itself.[20]

Laws on taxation not prescribed on a specific date of enforcement do not take effect until sixty days after their promulgation. This provision does not restrict the powers granted to the executive branch when acting under the extraordinary circumstances enumerated by the charter.[21]

Laws within the Venezuelan legislative system are directly subordinate to the constitution.[22]

TRATADO INTERNACIONAL (International Treaty). International treaties and agreements are negotiated by the president of the republic who also ratifies them after they are approved by an ordinary law.[23] The charter provides, however, that no law shall be required to approve an international instrument when it is issued to implement previous commitments of the state or apply expressly recognized principles, or when it simply requires the exercise of powers specifically granted to the executive branch by the constitution. In the latter case, the charter prescribes that a notification from the president to Congress concerning the international commitment is sufficient.[24]

No provisions were found in the charter or elsewhere concerning the rank of international treaties and agreements within the national legislative scheme. One must go by the general rule that all legislative and executive issuances must conform to the national charter.[25] Notwithstanding, a Venezuelan scholar briefly commenting on the topic stated that in view of the frequent conflicts between ordinary laws and international treaties, the general principle of positive law is observed whereby a special statute takes precedence over a general one, which makes the general laws subordinate to international instruments in some instances. Furthermore, the Venezuelan Code of Civil Procedure provides that in cases where the application of international private law norms is required, judges assign preference to the public treaties entered into by Venezuela.[26]

DECRETO (Decree). This is an instrument by which most of the administrative functions entrusted to the executive branch are performed. Most significantly, it is also the instrument by means of which the president exercises his regulatory powers to enforce and implement the national laws. Regulatory decrees must, of course, conform strictly to the laws they intend to regulate or implement, and ultimately to the constitution.[27]

Enforceability of decrees requires the observance of basic formalities for their issuance. They must be signed by the president of the republic and countersigned by one or more corresponding ministers of the cabinet; countersigning is waived when the president exercises such exclusive powers as appointing or removing a cabinet minister or acting as commander in chief of the armed forces.[28]

There are some special and extraordinary powers granted to the president of the republic under the Venezuelan charter which can critically affect a number of constitutional guarantees. Under certain circumstances, the president may declare the country in a state of emergency, establish, modify, or suppress public services, or take extraordinary measures vis-à-vis economic and financial matters.[29] Even though no information has been found regarding the specific instrument the president uses to impart orders, it is apparent that he does so by means of decrees. The opinion of experts is not completely clear concerning the charter's provision for these extraordinary powers. There are also a number of unanswered questions regarding the authority rank of decrees whose content is regulatory, which would make them subordinate to the laws they regulate, and those including provisions resulting from the direct exercise of extraordinary constitutional powers. The latter are more likely to be similar to the laws than the decrees.

Under the Venezuelan charter, decrees affecting constitutional guarantees which are issued by the executive under state of emergency do not interfere with the performance or the prerogatives of the other branches of government.[30] Furthermore, they are required to be submitted with the support of the Council of Ministers of the cabinet to the congressional chambers for consideration and approval. This legislative decision is made in a joint session or by the congressional delegated commission.

Since these decrees affect constitutional guarantees, they also have a direct restrictive impact on the related laws. It may therefore be suggested that decrees in this category issued under a state of emergency may eventually carry a force clearly stronger than that of the regulatory ones.

As stated by Venezuelan scholars, decrees in the area of financial and economic emergencies issued by the president under the specific powers granted by the constitution have the force of law and are commonly referred to as decree laws.[31]

Decrees concerning the establishment, modification, or suppression of public services may only be issued with the consent of the congressional delegated commission and if Congress is in recess. These decrees are also assigned higher ranking authority since, under ordinary circumstances, the area of legislation on public services is entrusted by the charter to the legislative chambers.

Finally, all decrees are inserted in the official gazette, another formal requirement for their enforceability.[32]

Notes

1. *Constitución* [January 23, 1961], *Gaceta Oficial* (*G.O.*) (May 11, 1973), Constitutional amendment no. 1 of May 9, 1973 (May 11, 1973), art. 215, nos. 3 and 6 (hereafter cited as *Const.*).
2. Ibid., art. 245, nos. 1 to 6.
3. Ibid., art. 246, nos. 1 to 4.
4. Ibid., arts. 248 and 175.
5. Ibid., arts. 138 and 139.
6. Ibid., art. 162.
7. Ibid., art. 163.
8. Ibid., art. 164.
9. Ibid., art. 165, nos. 1 to 5.
10. Ibid., art. 228.
11. Ibid., arts. 150, nos. 1 to 10; and 153, nos. 1 to 3.
12. Ibid., arts. 166 to 168.
13. Ibid., art. 171.
14. Ibid., art. 173, pars. 1 to 4.
15. Ibid., art. 173.
16. Ibid., art. 174.
17. Ibid., art. 175.
18. Ibid., art. 176.
19. Ibid., art. 177.
20. O. Lazo, *Código Civil de Venezuela, concordado y anotado,* 3rd ed. (Caracas: Ediciones Legis, 1965), art. 1 (hereafter cited as Lazo, *C. Civ.*).
21. *Const.*, art. 226.
22. Ibid., art. 215, nos. 3 and 6.
23. Ibid., art. 190, no. 5.
24. Ibid., art. 128.
25. Ibid., art. 215, nos. 3 and 6.
26. C. A. Tinoco Richter, *Teoría de la administración y del derecho administrativo* (Caracas: Universidad Central de Venezuela, 1970), p. 70 (hereafter cited as Tinoco, *Teoría*).
27. *Const.*, arts. 215, no. 6; and 190, nos. 1 to 10; Tinoco, *Teoría*, pp. 64 to 67.
28. *Const.*, art. 190.
29. Ibid., art. 190, nos. 6, 8, and 11.
30. Ibid., art. 241.
31. Tinoco, *Teoría,* p. 66; A. Moles Caubet, *Dogmática de los decretos leyes* (Caracas: Universidad Central de Venezuela, 1974), p. 23.
32. Law of Official Publications of July 22, 1941, in Lazo, *C. Civ.*, arts. 13 and 14, pp. 119 and 120.

☆ U.S. GOVERNMENT PRINTING OFFICE: 1979 O—273-955